THE STAIN AND SPOT REMOVER HANDBOOK

JEAN COOPER

A Storey Publishing Book

Storey Communications, Inc.
Schoolhouse Road
Pownal, Vermont 05261

The mission of Storey Communications is to serve our customers
by publishing practical information that encourages personal
independence in harmony with the environment.

Edited by Elizabeth McHale
Cover design by Cindy McFarland
Cover photograph by Nicholas Whitman
Text design and production by Meredith Maker
Production assistance by Susan Bernier
Indexed by Northwind Editorial Services

For Jennifer and Katherine, Bebbie and Marianne.

Copyright © Jean Cooper, 1995
Material in *The Stain and Spot Remover Handbook*
originally appeared in *Handy Household Hints,* © Jean Cooper, 1993
Little Hills Press Pty Ltd, Sydney, Australia

The information in this book is true and complete to the best of our knowledge. All recommendations are made without guarantee on the part of the author or Storey Communications, Inc. The author and publisher disclaim any liability in connection with the use of this information. For additional information please contact Storey Communications, Inc., Schoolhouse Road, Pownal, Vermont 05261.

Printed in the United States by R.R. Donnelley
10   9   8   7   6   5   4   3   2

Library of Congress Cataloging-in-Publication Data

Cooper, Jean. 1914–
      The stain and spot remover handbook / Jean Cooper.
              p.   cm.
      "A Storey Publishing book."
      Includes bibliographical references and index.
      ISBN 0-88266-811-0 (pbk.)
      1. Spotting (Cleaning)—Handbooks, manuals, etc. I. Title.
TX324.C66   1995
648'.1—dc20   95-12056
                                                                    CIP

Contents

Introduction

A wide range of laundry aids are available these days: pre-wash enzyme-soaking compounds, spray-on stain and grime removers, soaps and detergents, water softeners, fabric softeners, starches and stiffeners. And along with that there are many fibers — and blends of fibers, natural and synthetic — that require special handling. Care instructions now come in most garments, but extra information is needed to treat fibers that have become stained.

Similarly, our homes present the same challenge — an infinite combination of surfaces that best serve our purposes when they are clean. To be efficient with your time, you need information on how to apply the minimum effort to caring for and cleaning your home and belongings, and at the same time receive the maximum return.

The Stain and Spot Remover Handbook will tell you exactly how to clean your home and everything in it. It will tell you how to remove stains from just about any surface or material. It will give you tips on how to brighten and revive dull finishes, how to remove rust, how to make your own furniture polish, how to launder fragile curtains, how to avoid cleaning disasters.

The first section gives general stain removal advice. The second section describes all the various stain-removing agents (in alphabetical order) that are useful around the house and in the laundry room. The next section tells you how to clean everything in your house: carpets, curtains, wicker, wood, sinks, appliances, and so on. The last section is the last word on stain removal — it lists specific stains alphabetically and describes various methods for successfully treating and removing the

Organizing Your Care Labels

It may simplify the laundering of fine washables if you remove the care label, but remember to first identify the garment it goes with. Care labels often become unreadable after washing and cleaning, so this will keep the instructions easy to read. Use push pins or small hooks to hang these in a handy place in the laundry room. A bulletin board or a square piece of cork would be good for this.

Hang the extra buttons or mending thread/darning yarn from the same hook as the garment care label. That way, you will have no problem finding these things when you need them later.

stain. In the appendix, the reader will find a handy reference for hazardous materials that — while they may save a garment or revive a valued item with their potency — must be disposed of with care.

This book gives you all the stain removal and cleaning suggestions that we could fit in these pages. Many of the methods are old-fashioned, tried and true, ranging from mild to those you would use with caution.

We continue to work toward finding environmentally friendly solutions for use in our homes and in our lives, and reducing polluted waste water and exposure to harmful chemicals, but ultimately the one place we can control our environment is in our home.

Some manufacturers are now producing an all-natural cleaning vinegar, which is twice the strength of cooking vinegar. In time, there will be more organic, non-toxic products available for use in our homes. Yet right now, in our kitchens and in our pantries, there are endless materials we can use that are mild, organic, and safe. With *The Stain and Spot Remover Handbook,* you can put those products to good use.

Part One

GENERAL STAIN REMOVAL ADVICE

There are a few important points to keep in mind when working with stains and spills.

➤ Most stains will be easy to remove if they are treated while fresh.

➤ *Always* remove as much of the spill as possible before you start treating the stain. Work as gently as you can. Wringing or rubbing can cause a stain to penetrate more deeply. Lift the spilled material off gently with a spoon or butter knife. The more you can remove before you start treating the stain, the less the fabric will absorb.

➤ Start at the outer edges of the stain and work toward the center to avoid spreading the stain. Always blot; never scrub.

➤ Read and follow all directions before you start to work on removing a stain.

➤ Work methodically and patiently when removing a stain.

➤ Avoid staining other parts of the garment by stretching the stained section over an absorbent pad. Use an old towel and fold it over several times to absorb the stain as it dissolves.

➤ *Always* test the stain removal agent on the garment or surface you want to use it on. Test it in an inconspicuous place, such as the tail of a shirt or blouse or an inside seam or hem. If it was safe, and especially if it removed the stain, make a note of it somewhere. You may need to remove something similar from the same item in the future.

➤ Try the simplest approach first. Cold, clean water is a solvent that can remove many stains quickly, easily, and safely. Consider the fibers you are treating. (Even water can damage some textiles. Always check the garment care label.) See the section in this book on the particular textile and also on the particular stain.

➤ Purchase expensive solvents if necessary in order to remove a stain. If the garment is a good one and the stain is difficult to remove, take it to a drycleaner and describe the cause of the stain and what treatment, if any, you have tried, and point out the label showing the type of fibers involved.

➤ If the origin of the stain is unknown, try to determine if it is a greasy or nongreasy mark. If it is a protein stain (e.g., blood, grass, or egg), soak it in cold water.

➤ Air-dry items you have treated to be sure that the stain is completely gone. Some stains are not easily seen when the fabric is wet, and a hot dryer could set the stain and make it more difficult to remove.

GREASY STAINS

These can come from butter or margarine, oily foods, and automotive oil. Washable fabrics can be pre-treated by rubbing a little liquid detergent or drycleaning fluid directly on the spot. An old oil stain that has yellowed can be treated with bleach. For nonwashable fabrics, apply drycleaning fluid from the edges to the center of the stain. Allow the spot to dry completely before repeating. Another way to remove greasy stains from nonwashable fabrics is to use an absorbent substance, such as cornstarch, cornmeal, or chalk. Dust it on the greasy stain, wait until it looks caked, then brush it off gently.

NONGREASY STAINS

Nongreasy stains include fruit juice, black coffee, tea, ink. Nongreasy stains on washable fabrics should be sponged with cool water as soon as possible. Then soak the fabric in cool water for a few hours or overnight. If the stain is persistent, rub some liquid detergent directly into the area, then rinse with cool water. As a last resort, you may want to try color-safe bleach, but always check the manufacturer's care label.

A nongreasy stain on nonwashable fabric can be sponged with cool water. You will want to flush the stain: Place a clean, absorbent cloth behind the stain and apply cool water with an eye dropper or spray bottle. Your chance of succeeding in removing a nongreasy stain this way is greatest if the stain is fresh.

A Word of Caution

Never combine stain removal products, especially ammonia and chlorine bleach; it could generate dangerous fumes.

Treat flammable solvents with special care. Work in a well-ventilated room or on an outside patio. Do not smoke and do not work near a pilot light or open fire.

Air out rags or items thoroughly if they have been treated with a solvent-based product. Hang them outside where children and animals cannot get into them. Allow petroleum-based products to evaporate before putting the item of clothing through your washer.

Always dispose of used solvents or cleaning materials in accordance with your local hazardous waste regulations. (There is a hazardous waste chart at the end of this book. Use hazardous materials with caution and dispose of them properly.)

If water does not remove the stain on washable fabric, apply liquid detergent to the stained fabric and rinse the area with cool water. After you have rinsed the area and completely removed detergent residue, sponge the spot with rubbing alcohol.

COMBINATION STAINS

When you have a combination of greasy and nongreasy stains (e.g., coffee with cream, lipstick), first deal with the nongreasy stain. With washable fabrics, first sponge the stain with cool water, then apply liquid detergent to the stain and rinse well. Let the fabric air dry, then deal with the greasy stain: Apply drycleaning fluid to the stain and allow it to dry. If the stain is not gone, reapply drycleaning fluid.

Part Two

STAIN REMOVAL AGENTS

ABSORBENTS

Use clean white cloths to absorb spills on fabric. It is easier to see how much of the spill is being absorbed if the material is white. Tissues, blotting paper, and sponges are all good choices.

Blot and reblot fresh spills until no more stain can be absorbed. Avoid rubbing — this will spread the stain. When the spill is completely absorbed, treat the stain. (Part Four lists specific stains in alphabetical order.)

Absorbent powders. Absorbing agents include powdered starch, talcum powder, powdered chalk, cornstarch, and potato flour.

Sprinkle the powder over the damp spill. As the powder absorbs the spill and dries, brush it off or use the vacuum cleaner hose to remove it. Repeat until no more stain can be absorbed. Absorbent powders are good grease absorbers.

ACETONE

Acetone is the basic ingredient in nail polish remover, but nail polish remover may contain other substances that can make a stain worse. A concentrated form of acetone can be used to remove stains such as ballpoint ink and household cement.

Spread the stained area over a pad, cover it with a few drops of acetone, and scrub gently with a butter knife. Discard the pad when it becomes discolored and repeat the process.

Rub the stained area with powdered detergent, then rinse under hard-running cold water. If the remainder of the stain does not wash out, wash it in color-safe bleach if the garment care label lists it as safe.

Recommendations: Flammable and poisonous. Do not use on acetate. Test before using on natural or synthetic fibers.

Availability: Drugstores

ALCOHOL *(isopropyl alcohol, a 70 percent solution)*

Alcohol can be very helpful in removing some kinds of stains, but if you are working with acetate, acrylic, rayon, or vinyl, you will need to dilute the rubbing alcohol with water (1 part alcohol to 2 parts water). Denatured alcohol (a 90 percent solution) can also be used.

Recommendations: Flammable. May cause some dyes to fade; test an inconspicuous area of the garment first.

Availability: Grocery stores, drugstores

AMMONIA

Ammonia is a colorless gas made up of nitrogen and hydrogen. It is easily absorbed by water. Sold in diluted form, it works well on many surfaces and materials as a deodorizer and cleanser. It is a good grease cutter, wax stripper, and soil remover. Ammonia can restore color altered by contact with acids.

Recommendations: Never mix ammonia and chlorine bleach; the combination produces toxic fumes. Do not use in a confined space; the fumes are strong.

May cause some dyes to fade, so test it on the fabric

Ammonia — Cleaning Tips
For washing windows, use ½ cup of ammonia in a gallon of water. To make oven cleaning easier, place a saucer of ammonia inside a cool oven overnight, then wipe out and clean the next day. **Note:** Do not use ammonia on a self-cleaning oven. Refer instead to the manufacturer's instructions.

first. Ammonia is generally not safe for use on silk or wool. If an article changes color as a result of the application of ammonia, quickly rinse the affected area with water that has a few drops of vinegar added to it; rinse thoroughly.
Availability: Grocery stores

BAKING SODA *(sodium bicarbonate)*

Baking soda is a cheap, nonabrasive cleanser and deodorizer. It can be used as a mild scouring powder or mixed with water to create a paste for cleaning dirty surfaces.
Availability: Grocery stores

BLEACHES. *See Ammonia, Chlorine Bleach, Hydrogen Peroxide, Lemon Juice, Powdered Bleaches, Sunlight, Vinegar*

Bleaching agents are helpful in treating stains and reducing the natural yellowing of fabrics. If bleaching is necessary, choose a type of bleach that suits the fabric.

BORAX

Borax is used to remove fruit, tea, and coffee stains; to remove tannin from teapots and coffee makers; and to soften hard water. As a paste, it can be used to remove stains from carpets.

CHLORINE BLEACH

Chlorine bleach can be used on white cottons, linens, and synthetic fabrics. It can remove stains but it does weaken fibers if it stays on fabrics for too long. Chlorine bleach should not be used on silk, wool, or fabrics that are exposed to sunlight. You must dilute chlorine bleach before adding it to the washer, and rinse articles thoroughly. Failure to do this can cause discoloration and can even leave holes in fabrics.
Recommendations: Wear rubber gloves and avoid inhaling the fumes. Never mix bleach with ammonia or any

Chlorine Precautions

☞ Do not use metal containers when soaking articles in bleach; use china, glass, porcelain, enamel, or plastic.

☞ Chlorine bleach is poisonous. Contact with skin or eyes can cause burns and irritation.

☞ Never mix bleach with any other cleaning materials except laundry detergent. Combining bleach with strong acids or alkalis can produce deadly gases.

ammonia-based cleaners. Use only in well-ventilated areas.

Availability: Grocery stores

CITRIC ACID. *See also Lemon Juice*

Some stain removers on the market contain citric acid. The ones that also contain petroleum distillates are a combination of solvent and bleaching agent.

Recommendation: Always test the solution first. Use products with petroleum derivatives in well ventilated area.

Availability: Grocery stores, drugstores

DETERGENTS

Liquid and powdered detergents are often successful in removing fresh stains from washable clothing.

Granular vs. Liquid Detergents

Granular detergents generally remove mud and clay better than liquid detergents. Liquid detergents are preferable for cleaning greasy or oily stains. Some products may contain added enzymes or bleaching agents for stain removal.

Make a paste of powdered detergent and water or rub undiluted liquid dishwashing detergent directly onto the stain. Scrub the area between two fingers. Rinse by holding the stained area taut under cold running water. Then turn the fabric over and treat the reverse side.

If stain removal directions call for liquid laundry detergent to be applied directly to the stain, check the manufacturer's label. Not all liquid laundry detergents are safe to apply directly to fabric.

DYE STRIPPERS

Dye strippers invariably entail the use of boiling water, which can damage crease-resistant and treated fabrics, woolens, and other materials. But for articles that can tolerate boiling water, dye strippers can be used effectively.
Recommendations: Follow manufacturer's directions.
Availability: Hardware stores

EUCALYPTUS

Eucaluptus is widely cultivated for its gums, resins, and oil. It can be useful in cutting through some kinds of grease.
Recommendations: Test first in an inconspicuous area. Blot frequently as you work.
Availability: Drugstores

FURNITURE POLISH

Read the labels carefully before purchasing a furniture polish to make sure the polish is the best for your purpose. Beeswax polishes preserve and enhance the finish on solid woods. They are excellent for use on light woods where the use of oily polishes would darken the grain. Oil-based polishes are good for dark woods. Apply sparingly on a slighly dampened cloth and polish with a dry duster.
Recommendation: Do not use oil-based polishes if a synthetic finish has been applied to the wood.
Availability: Grocery stores

GLYCERIN

Glycerin is an ingredient in many solvents on the market today. Used alone, it is a weak solvent but a good pre-soaking agent for some stains.
Availability: Drugstores

HOT WATER

Water that is 140° F or hotter, in general, provides the most soil removal and sanitizing, especially of white cottons, linens, and heavily soiled cottons that are colorfast.

Recommendations: Reduces the resilience of synthetic fibers; may cause some colors to run.

HYDROGEN PEROXIDE

Hydrogen peroxide (3 percent strength) is a safe and handy stain remover. For white fabrics (except some rayons and white nylon), to 1 part of 3 percent peroxide add 3 parts of warm water, ¼ teaspoon of white vinegar, and 1 drop of ammonia. Soak stain for 10 minutes, then rinse well. Repeat as necessary.

Recommendations: Buy peroxide in small quantities to make sure it is fresh — it loses strength as it ages or if it is exposed to light. (Check the expiration date on the label.)

Availability: Grocery stores, drugstores

KEROSENE

Kerosene has been used for years to remove hard-water stains in tubs and sinks, and for wiping down tiles.

Recommendations: Flammable and toxic; use with caution.

Availability: Hardware stores

LEMON JUICE. *See also Citric Acid*

Lemon juice is a bleaching agent that is good for lightening ivory (such as ivory piano keys), removing some stains, and deodorizing.

MOTHBALLS AND MOTHFLAKES

The special mothproofing process for blankets and garments employed by drycleaners is not available for domestic use. Synthetic fabrics are not vulnerable to moths; only woolen materials require mothproofing. But if thoroughly clean woolens are stored in pest-free surroundings, they will be protected. Mothballs and -flakes should never be in direct contact with woolens; enclose them in an old handkerchief or a cloth bag.

NAVAL JELLY

Naval jelly removes rust stains instantly.
Recommendations: Wear gloves to protect the skin.
Availability: Hardware stores

OXALIC ACID

Oxalic acid is a poisonous substance sold in crystal form. It is extremely useful for removing rust from metals.
Recommendations: Oxalic acid is poisonous and must be handled with care. Contact your local hazardous waste authority for proper disposal. Wear gloves and keep out of the reach of children and pets.
Availability: Can be special-ordered at drugstores

PETROLEUM JELLY

Petroleum jelly can be used as a pre-solvent for difficult grease or oil stains, but after it dissolves the stain you will need to treat the remaining discoloration with an additional degreasing solution.

POWDERED BLEACHES

Powdered bleaches are a good substitute when chlorine bleach cannot be used. When using powdered bleaches, make a paste with water and powder and apply to damp fabric. Rinse thoroughly with cool water any time you use a bleaching agent.

POWDERS. *See Absorbents, Detergents, Scouring Powders*

SCOURING POWDERS

Scouring powders come in many heavy-duty varieties: Some are good for rust spots on cast iron; others are good for sinks, bathtubs, and so on; and various softscrub cleaners are available for your fiberglass, Formica, and stainless steel surfaces.

SOAP

Bar soap is sometimes called for in stain removal directions. Do not use bath soaps that contain added moisturizers, fragrances, dyes, or deodorants. These added ingredients can themselves sometimes cause stains.

SOLVENTS. *See also Acetone*

Many cleaning products contain solvents. For example, turpentine is a solvent: It dissolves paint and grease. Water is also a solvent, but it is not a hazardous one. Most organic solvents are highly flammable and poisonous.

Common organic solvents are petroleum distillates, trichloroethane, mineral spirits, carbon tetrachloride, and methylene chloride. Many materials you might use in stain removal, such as nail polish removers, paint thinners, drycleaning fluids, and degreasers, contain almost 100 percent solvent.

If you have applied a solvent to an item of clothing, place that item outdoors — away from children or pets — and allow the solvent to evaporate before washing the item.

Clothing treated with solvent-containing products should be completely dry before you wear them.

If you want to know more about a particular solvent, contact the manufacturer of the product (your local library should be able to locate the address or telephone number). Your Cooperative Extension Service is also a good source of information. Contact local poison centers for information on health effects.

Some people are extremely sensitive to solvents such as petroleum distillates.

If it is necessary to buy a special solvent or if you are in doubt about your ability to treat a difficult stain, send the article to a drycleaner. The incorrect use of a solvent might damage the material and cause a worse stain than the original. Some solvents can remove dyes or finish from a material or actually damage the fabric.

Drycleaning fluids will remove most greasy stains. Apply in small amounts. Several light applications are more effective than one large one.

Work over an old folded towel. Place the stained side face down and work from the back of it so that the stain will be washed out of the fabric. Change the absorbent pad under the material as it becomes soiled so that loosened stain elements will not restain the fabric.

Recommendations: Use with caution; fumes are toxic and cumulative, particularly if the user has been drinking alcohol (alcohol can make solvents more toxic to the user). Some are flammable, so do not work near a fire or flame and do not smoke. Work in a well-ventilated area, and do not inhale the fumes.

Solvent Precaution

Avoid wearing contact lenses when using solvents because the vapors can get trapped between your eye and the lens.

Disposing of Solvents

Because they can be environmentally hazardous, use solvent-containing products conservatively. Used paint thinner can be strained and reused. Always follow your local solid waste authority's recommendations for disposing of unused cleaning solvents. (See Appendix for Hazardous Waste Disposal.)

SUNLIGHT. *See Bleaches*

Sometimes bleaching can be achieved by natural means. For instance, fine lace, which could be weakened by commercial bleaches, can be bleached by sunlight. Carefully tack the lace to a sheet and suspend the sheet between three or four clotheslines overnight. Repeat if necessary.

To whiten a discolored article, dampen it and place it in strong sunlight. Gradually it should whiten.

Recommendations: Some fibers may be weakened by sunlight.

TURPENTINE

Turpentine is a solvent that is used as a thinner for oil-based paints. It is also very effective on paint and grease stains where the textile can tolerate turpentine.

VINEGAR

White vinegar is a solution of 5 percent acetic acid. Dilute before using on cotton or linen. Vinegar can change the color of some dyes, so it should always be tested first.

WASHING SODA *(sodium carbonate)*

Washing soda, or "sal soda," is sodium carbonate and can be used to help cut grease and soften water. Add it to your regular laundry: use 4 tablespoons (60 ml) to a load of wash, and cut back on the amount of detergent. Use more washing soda for heavily soiled clothes.

Recommendations: Do not use on silk or wool.

Availability: Grocery stores and drugstores

Part Three

CLEANING EVERYTHING IN YOUR HOUSE

ACETATES

Acetate is used for curtains; for evening fabrics such as brocades, taffetas, and satin; and for lining materials. Do not allow acetates to become very dirty. Wash frequently in cool detergent suds. Swirl about in the water but do not rub, wring, or twist. Rinse well; press with a low-set iron while still slightly damp.

ALUMINUM

Aluminum is widely used for cookware, and in different gauges it can be adapted for various uses. Heavy gauge saucepans with milled bases do not buckle with heat, and they rest flat on electric hot plates. Aluminum cake pans are easy to clean, and they are nonrusting.

This metal will stain easily, however, if it is exposed to any alkali, even to salt or soda; but contrary to popular belief, the stains are not harmful. They can be removed in a number of ways:

1. Scrub the utensil with well-soaped fine steel wool pads.
2. Boil apple peelings or citrus skins in the pan.
3. Add 2 teaspoons (10 ml) of cream of tartar per quart (liter) of cold water in a stained saucepan. Bring the water to boiling point and simmer for three minutes. Discard the water and polish with a soapy steel wool pad.

Aluminum teapots. The outside of an aluminum teapot can be polished with fine steel wool. Rinse under a running tap. Shake off the droplets of water that remain. Do not wipe dry.

To remove tannin stains from the inside of an aluminum teapot, fill it with boiling water and add ¼ cup (60 ml) borax. Let the solution stand in the pot until it is cold, then scrub the inside of the pot with a nylon brush. Do not use a pot scraper for this job; it could weaken thin aluminum and cause pinpricks, which will leak.

Push a pipe cleaner through tannin-clogged spout holes, working from the inside of the teapot and up the spout. Rinse well by forcing water from a running tap through the holes.

Aluminum saucepans. A burnt aluminum saucepan can be treated in several ways. Try to avoid chipping and scraping; the resultant scars will attract stains that will be difficult to remove later. Scrape out as much of the burnt food as possible with a wooden spoon or a firm plastic or rubber spatula. Then expose the dry pot to hot sunshine for at least a week, keeping it dry at night. Day by day some of the burnt food will flake off when nudged with a spatula. Then boil undiluted household bleach and a teaspoonful (5 ml) of borax in the pan, using an amount sufficient to cover the stain. Finally, polish the area with steel wool, and after rinsing thoroughly, return the pan to regular use. The remaining black flecks will gradually disappear. They are not detrimental to health.

Once badly burnt, an aluminum saucepan will easily burn again. Reconstitute it by rubbing the inside with unsalted fat, such as lard, and heat the pan very gently before using it.

Aluminum frying pans and the inside of deep-fry cookers often become very stained with burnt-on grease. There are commercial cleaners on the market, and these should be used according to instructions as they are highly corrosive.

ANGORA

This is a wool made from rabbit fur or goat hair. Sometimes angora is blended with nylon, and this sheds less fluff than does pure angora.

Wash in lukewarm water with a well-whisked wool-washing liquid soap compound or mild soap flakes. Knead the garment under water. Do not rub or twist or lift it out of the water; the weight of the water can cause undue stretching. If possible, wash in a sink or tub so that the plug can be released to let out the washing and subsequent rinsing waters. Simply press the garment to extract the water. After rinsing, place the garment on a towel, mold it into shape, fold in the ends of the towel, and roll the garment in its folds. Dry flat on a sheet on the lawn, or over newspaper and a sheet on a clean cement surface, out of direct sunlight. Turn to dry the underside. Shake well when dry to raise the furry nap. Do not press. If wrinkles appear, simply hold a steaming iron just above the garment.

APPLIANCES

Keep all booklets and warranties together in a plastic bag for easy reference. The date of purchase and the model number could be required in case of an insurance claim or if repairs are necessary.

Always switch off the electricity before attempting to clean an appliance. Cleaning with water can cause short circuits and prove life-threatening if the power is left on.

BABY ITEMS

Baby clothing. Baby skin can become irritated by harsh detergents. Dissolve mild soap flakes well in lukewarm water before immersing baby garments. Rinse twice. Dry inside out in a semi-shaded area. Fine woolens will scorch in direct sunlight.

Plastic and waterproof pants. Wash frequently after rinsing or pre-soaking to remove traces of soiling or ammonia. Use lukewarm suds and soap flakes or very mild detergent. Dry inside out.

Diapers. Borax, long acclaimed as an excellent deodorizer and cleaner for baby (and geriatric) garments, is slightly cheaper than the soaking compounds. Borax or one of the compounds should be used as a soaking agent to counteract odor and traces of ammonia and to keep the diapers white.

An integral part of nursery equipment is a large plastic bucket with a lid. Once a day put 2 rounded tablespoons (30 ml) of your preferred soaking compound in the bottom of the bucket and add 7 quarts (liters) of cold water. Put in wet diapers as they are changed; dispose of heavy soiling before soaking other diapers. Leave for several hours or overnight.

Once a day empty the contents of the bucket into a tub and let the soaking water drain away. Flush the diapers with tap water and drain again. Now the diapers will be clean enough to be washed with other baby things such as sheets, pillowcases, and cotton undershirts that will withstand the use of hot water. Do not add woolens or drip-dry fabrics. Woolens will shrink in hot water and drip-dry garments will crease badly. Instead, these should be hand-washed in cool suds.

Use the hot-water cycle and soap flakes or a mild liquid detergent in the washing machine to wash the diapers and cotton articles. For economy's sake, use a cold-water rinse if the machine can be adjusted.

The two rinse cycles of the average automatic machine will adequately remove all traces of ammonia, soap, or detergent. Never use heavy-duty detergents to wash babywear. Residues can cause chafing and rashes.

If the water is hard, liquid detergent is preferable; and to dispel any traces (urine, soap, or detergent) use borax or fabric softener (occasionally, according to directions on the package) to make the diapers and garments soft and fluffy.

Dry the diapers in the sun whenever possible and fold them so they will be ready for use. Correctly laundered diapers prevent chafing and rashes, resulting in a more contented, comfortable baby.

Bassinet and crib sheets, blankets, towels, and washrags. Pre-soak to remove soil stains. Wash in water at a temperature suitable to the fabric. Use a very mild detergent or soap flakes. Thorough rinsing is necessary; ammonia in urine can react on traces of detergent and cause chafing and skin rashes.

Hand-knitted baby clothes. Hand-wash in lukewarm water using a mild soap powder or liquid. Rinse thoroughly. Roll in a towel to extract extra moisture. Dry in semi-shade out of direct sunlight to avoid yellowing.

To store baby clothing, wash and rinse well; dry thoroughly. Age and damp conditions can cause brown spots to appear; stains should be removed or they will become brown and impossible to treat.

Baby toys. Stuffed toys lose their pristine appearance after a few months of rough and tumble, and to keep them hygienic and attractive they must be cleaned or washed.

Not all fluffy toys are washable, however. Some have fillings that will swell and burst seams or disintegrate when immersed in water. It is important to check the care label on toys to see if they are washable, either by hand or in a machine, and whether machine drying is permitted.

When children become very attached to particular toys, it is often difficult to withdraw them even for a day for cleaning, let alone discard them because they are shabby.

Soft, stuffed pastel-colored and white toys that have been lightly soiled can be freshened by dusting them heavily with baby powder, powdered starch, or cornstarch. Work the powder into the pile with fingertips.

Roll the toys in the folds of a towel and leave them for several hours — overnight if the toys can be spared.

Have a freshly washed and dried clothes brush ready. Working outside, thoroughly brush the pile to remove the powder.

Wash and press any ribbon trimming, or apply new ribbon to give a cleaner look to much-handled fluffy toys.

If the care label so states, many toys, including some teddy bears, are washable in cool, mild detergent suds.

Rinse well, squeeze out as much water as possible, then run the toys through the spin cycle of the washing machine with two dry towels. The friction will fluff up the toy and drying can then be completed in open air.

Use a piece of toweling with a good texture, or a toothbrush dipped in soapy water to brush and wipe soiled synthetic fur. Then wipe the fur with a damp cloth and dry again.

Plastic rattles, teethers, and similar toys, which often find themselves in babies' mouths, should be washed regularly in hot soapy water or in the dishwasher. Rinse thoroughly.

Safety Regulations
Safety regulations are now quite strict regarding eyes, bells, and other such parts on stuffed toys, but it is advisable to test them from time to time, and certainly after the toys have been washed, to ensure that they have not loosened.

BATHROOM FIXTURES

Bathtub and sink. Stains caused by spilled hair dyes, medicines, and cosmetics can often be removed by the application of a paste made of cream of tartar and peroxide. Smear it on heavily and let it dry for 3 hours. Rinse off, and repeat if necessary, using a fresh paste.

Put 10 tablespoons (150 ml) of cold water in a spray bottle. Add 1 tablespoon (15 ml) of acetic acid (vinegar) to the water. Spray about ½ square yard (0.5 square meter) at a time, beginning at the bottom and working upward. Leave the spray on for a minute. Wipe off with clean water. When the job is finished, wipe all over with clean water containing 1 tablespoon (15 ml) of washing soda to neutralize the acid.

A cracked bathroom sink can be patched until a replacement is possible. Work from the underside. Wash the length of the crack to remove traces of grease and soap. Then stretch a length of wide waterproof adhesive plaster along the length of the crack and smooth out all air bubbles.

Apply a coat of white paint and, when this dries, apply a second coat. Do not use the sink for 24 hours. Meanwhile use epoxy porcelain mender, obtainable at a hardware store, to fill in any chips on the inside of the sink.

Rust marks on a bathtub or sink can be rubbed hard with a cloth dipped in undiluted vinegar. Or wipe the rust marks off instantly with an application of naval jelly. It is available in some hardware stores, and it is worth the effort to acquire a bottle. Wear gloves to protect the skin.

Bathroom tiles. To clean the grouting around the tub and shower, use any thick emulsion cleaner as a temporary grout between tiles. Spread a few drops on with a fingertip and let it dry. Later, clean tiles to remove traces of dried emulsion.

Bathroom mirrors. To prevent a bathroom mirror from becoming clouded with steam, rub it all over with a cloth slightly dampened with glycerin.

The silver backing (which, by the way, is pure silver) can be affected by the use of and the method of application

Keeping Sponges Fresh
Loofahs and other natural sponges are excellent for removing scaly skin, but they tend to become slimy with soap unless they are cleaned regularly. First, rinse them under a running cold water tap, then soak them for an hour in cold vinegar water — 2 tablespoons (30 ml) per quart (liter).

of certain cleaners. Even the spray-on commercial window and glass cleaners, when applied to mirrors, should not be sprayed too liberally or be left on the surface for too long. It is safer to spray a soft cloth with the cleaner and apply that to the mirror.

A napless soft cloth wrung out of lukewarm liquid detergent suds will effectively clean mirrors. Or use ammonia water, 1 tablespoon (15 ml) to 1½ quarts (liters) of warm water. (See Mirrors)

Bathroom scales. These tend to rust with steam and dampness. Spray the metal parts with a rust inhibitor, or rub them lightly with petroleum jelly. Occasionally test the accuracy of the scales by weighing an article of marked weight, preferably one that weighs in excess of six or seven pounds. Adjust accordingly.

Shower curtains. These can be washed by hand or machine in warm suds. Warm water keeps plastic pliable.

Diluted bleach will remove most mold, mildew, and soap stains on shower curtains. The double benefit in soaking the curtain in the bathtub, of course, is that both will be cleaned. Stained white towels and other white cotton garments (not woolens, rayons, or silks) can be soaked at the same time.

Shower heads. These become clogged with mineral deposits after years of use. If possible, remove the head and scrub the inside with a ball of steel wool wrapped around a clothespin. If the head cannot be removed, scrub the underside with a sharp nylon brush or prick the holes with a darning needle. The removal of the shower head makes it possible to shake out loose grit that will reclog the holes.

BED LINEN

Sheets and pillowcases. Mend tears and patch weak sections before washing in a machine. Wash in hot water with good laundry detergent. Dry in full sunshine and fold as you take it from the clothesline.

Bedspreads. Washable spreads should be laundered according to the instructions on the care label. Nylon, polyester, or polyester-blend fibers and cottons wash well, but rayons, silks, and acetates require drycleaning.

Chenille spreads are excellent for use on children's beds, and they are easily washed in a machine, using hot detergent suds. Rinse twice and double the bedspread over a line to dry, with the wrong side uppermost so that the tufts rub against each other in the breeze, thus raising their nap. Chenille quilts often have a lint problem when new, but this abates after a few launderings. After washing, when the quilt is on the bed, a very light application of hair spray or spray-on starch will help to control loose fibers that cause lint collection. Clean out the washing machine filter thoroughly after washing these spreads.

Blankets. Woolen blankets can be hand- or machine-washed if you use cold water and mild or wool-washing detergent. In machine washing, use the shortest possible cycle. Wash one blanket at a time in plenty of water and rinse well. Spin drying or mechanical wringing will ensure quicker drying; this is important for woolen blankets. Blankets made of synthetic fibers will not shrink, but to keep them soft and fluffy, use a very cool wash and mild detergent or soap flakes.

Some synthetic blankets will discolor if exposed to full sunlight, so choose a windy day and dry in semi shade.

Dry blankets in an electric dryer on the low setting or over two clotheslines to permit the circulation of air between overhangs. Some woolen blankets become odorous when exposed to harsh sunlight, so dry these on a windy day in semi-shade also.

When blankets are dry, shake them vigorously to raise the nap. Press satin bindings with a very cool iron and store them in plastic bags or in new pillowcases, with moth deterrent if the blankets are made of wool. Synthetic blankets are mothproof.

BOOKS

To remove grease spots from old book covers, use an art gum eraser or fresh white bread (ball it up like a gum eraser). Dust on talcum powder, leave it on for a few hours, and wipe clean.

To clean grease, mold, or mildew from cloth bindings, try a thin paste of cornstarch and a cleaning fluid (experiment first on a spot of the binding that doesn't show too much, as discoloration sometimes results).

BRASS

The warmth and richness of well-polished brass adequately repays the time spent in maintaining its shine. Most homes have some brass objects. Ornaments can be cleaned, then clear-lacquered to maintain their glow and to cut down on work. The lacquer will last for months, depending on the amount of handling and the use the article receives, as well as climatic conditions. It is seldom worthwhile lacquering a brass tray that is regularly used because the surface will soon be abraded and the protective layer of lacquer will gradually flake off.

Church brasses are ideal candidates for lacquering. Some firms specialize in this type of lacquering. The only cleaning necessary is regular dusting with a soft cloth sprayed with silicone polish.

Many new brass articles are lacquered before they are sold, but thoroughly cleaned brass articles are easily sprayed at home. Purchase clear lacquer in an aerosol can for easy application, and follow the instructions on the label.

Neglected brass becomes almost black. If mild cleaners (such as brass polish, a cut lemon dipped in salt, or a mixture of vinegar and salt) prove ineffective, soak the item in a citric acid solution. Use a 1-ounce (25 g) packet of citric acid dissolved in 3½ quarts (liters) of hot (but not boiling) water in a nonmetal container. Use more solution if the article is large.

Soak for five minutes, then gently scrub etchings, ornamentation, or engravings with an old, soft toothbrush. Rinse under a running hot water tap, pat dry, and polish in the usual way.

This method of cleaning is ideal for Eastern brasses that are often deeply etched or inlaid.

An intermediate rubbing with a cloth dampened with cloudy ammonia will brighten unlacquered brass articles. The cloth will become quite black; check it frequently to ensure that you are polishing with a clean section of the cloth. Ammonia will also remove traces of polish embedded in etched brass objects. Do not immerse painted brassware.

When green or blue deposits build up on brass, a different treatment is necessary. Small, solid brass articles can be boiled in water containing washing soda: ½ cup (125 ml) soda to 1½ quarts (liters) water. Larger articles can be sponged with the solution. Small traces of deposits can often be rubbed off with a cloth dampened with vinegar or lemon juice sprinkled with salt. Rinse, wash, rinse again, dry, and polish.

Ornamental brass attached to canvas, leather, or to doors or cabinets requires careful cleaning if the base material is not to be stained by polish. Fine wood or cigarette ash can be used to polish the brass without damage to the base, or cardboard shields can be cut to slip under the brass ornament to be cleaned. After cleaning, apply clear lacquer.

The inside of brass cooking utensils must *not* be cleaned with polish. Instead, rub with vinegar or lemon juice and salt. If necessary, polish with a well-soaped pad of fine steel wool. Rinse under a running tap; wash in hot detergent suds, and rinse again. Keep these utensils thoroughly dry when not in use.

Commercial brass polishes are nonabrasive and will not cause scratches — providing the surface has first been dusted with a soft cloth to remove gritty deposits.

It is best to rub off the polish before it dries completely. Use a fresh cloth, for the cleaning pad will be black with metal deposits and grime.

BRONZE

Items made of a combination of copper and tin need little maintenance. Dust with a slightly oily cloth or with silicone polish to preserve their soft luster.

Neglected bronze should be washed in hot detergent suds. Use a soft brush to remove dust and grime. Rinse and dry, and finish off with an oily cloth or with silicone cream.

Candle Tips

☞ When setting new candles into candlesticks, dip the bases in hot water for a few seconds and push them firmly into position.

☞ Candles will burn longer if they are chilled in a refrigerator before being lit.

☞ Save candle ends to rub drawer runners and inside window frames to make windows and drawers run smoothly.

CANDLESTICK HOLDERS

Clean candlestick holders with the appropriate polish: Silver should be cleaned with silver polish, brass with brass polish. Crystal and glass can be washed in water containing ammonia. Wipe lacquered metals with a damp cloth and spray with silicone wax.

Old candle wax can be removed from candlesticks more easily if the wax is warmed. Leave the sticks in hot sunlight, train a hair dryer on them, or dip them in hot water for a few minutes. Ease off the softened wax with a blunt knife.

CARPETS

Act quickly when something has spilled on a carpet. Prompt attention and using correct solvents and cleaning methods is invariably more successful than belated attention by a professional carpet cleaner.

Don't panic! Use any dry colorfast absorbent material that is handy — a handkerchief, a cloth, tissues, or towels. The stain is more easily removed from these washable cloths than from the carpet. Do not rub; simply blot, using a series of fresh tissues or cloths until no more can be absorbed. Then treat the stain according to its nature.

Emergency Care Kit for Carpets

Keep these simple cleaning solutions handy:

- ☞ Powdered laundry detergent. Do not use liquid detergent.
- ☞ Tissues or clean absorbent dustrags. Old dish towels are excellent.
- ☞ A bottle of drycleaning solvent. This is flammable. Observe safety precautions.
- ☞ Paint thinner or acetone.
- ☞ Carpet-cleaning powder, which both cleans and deodorizes.
- ☞ An old clean toothbrush; borax; white vinegar; and household bleach.

For solid stains such as grease or food, use a kitchen spatula or pliable knife to scrape up as much as possible, then treat the remaining stain appropriately.

Note the telephone number of a reliable carpet-cleaning firm. Don't hesitate to call for help if the stain is a bad one.

Avoid excessive wetting. Water can *cause* a stain if it penetrates the backing and dissolves deep down dirt.

Do not tread on a damp carpet. Dry the area as quickly as possible with a fan, creating cross-ventilation, or use a hand-held hair dryer on a low setting. *Never* use a radiator.

When the stain has been treated, smooth the treated area so that it will dry as it should.

Bathroom carpets. Light-colored, rubber-backed bathroom carpeting soon becomes soiled from frequent traffic.

Synthetic floor coverings can be shampooed in place or taken up and cleaned in the washing machine.

Some drycleaners will accept these rugs, but they should be washed, not drycleaned, because the cleaning fluids can damage the rubber backing.

Some bathroom-sized carpets will fit into a large domestic washing machine. First vacuum the carpet well while it is still on the floor, then spray the soiled area with a pre-wash spray to loosen stubborn stains.

Set the machine for a short cycle using a full-load cold water supply and a cold water detergent. Hot water is detrimental to the rubber backing. Put the detergent in the bottom of the machine, not over the rug, which should be rolled loosely with the rubber backing in and the pile out. Arrange the rug evenly in the machine so as not to unbalance the load.

When the wash cycle is completed, spread the rug, pile side up, over three lines. Rubber-backed rugs should not be exposed to dryer heat.

When the carpet is quite dry, re-lay it and spray it with fabric protector to keep it cleaner longer.

Indoor-outdoor carpets. This type of carpet is generally stain-, mildew-, and rot-resistant. It is available in a wide range of patterns and colors and is ideal for use in schools, around pools, and on patios. No underfelt is required because the carpet and tiles are foam-backed.

The carpet can be loose-laid and affixed with a special carpet tape, or the clean, dry floor can be covered with adhesive and the carpet affixed.

Regular cleaning will make the carpet last longer and look better. Vacuum, hose, or sweep the carpet frequently, particularly if it is exposed to tracked-on sand and dirt.

Allow felt-type carpets to dry before walking on them. The wet surface can easily scuff, particularly from rubber-soled shoes.

Blot up spills and stains as soon as they occur. Make up a jar of laundry detergent suds — 1 tablespoon (15 ml) to one cup (250 ml) of water — and use this to sponge spots. Remove the suds with a series of clean, damp cloths.

Greasy stains might require special treatment with a solvent, but do not use spot removers or ammoniated cleaners on carpets containing vinyl.

Dilute drycleaning fluid with an equal amount of cold water to remove greasy marks, then test the solution on an inconspicuous part of the carpet.

Indoor-outdoor carpet is susceptible to burns from cigarette ash, barbecue fires, and so on. Although some

Carpet Cleaning with Foam and Powder Shampoo

There are several drycleaning powders on the market that absorb grease and grime in the carpet pile. Several hours after application, vacuum the powder; both powder and grime will lift away together.

Powder shampoo is an excellent stain absorber if it is applied as soon as spills have been blotted up. Work the powder into the stained area with a special appliance (often sold with the powder) or with a firm-bristled clean brush.

When vacuuming up the powder, work first across the pile and then in the opposite direction, slowly and methodically, so that no trace remains.

For regular cleaning, use about 1 oz. (25 g) per square yard (meter) — more if the area is deeply soiled. Leave it on for at least 20 minutes; several hours is preferable.

The use of shampoo powder avoids the problem of overwetting the carpet; and after vacuuming, the carpet can be walked on without having to wait for it to dry.

such fibers might not be dangerously flammable, they are sensitive to heat and will melt, leaving indelible stains.

Woolen carpets. Wool fibers have particularly good resilience. That is, having been walked upon, they bounce back. They do not burst into flame, but instead burn slowly with a telltale odor, which is an alarm itself. Provided spills are treated without delay, wool fibers are fairly resistant to most stains. Deeper stains usually respond to more concentrated treatment.

Woolen carpets need to be mothproofed to protect them against carpet beetles, silverfish, and moths.

Tests show that **nylon carpets** wear best of all. They soil easily but they can be cleaned without difficulty.

Acrylic carpets also wear well and maintain their appearance, despite heavy traffic. They soil quickly but are easy to clean. Choose a stippled or sculptured pattern to camouflage day-to-day soiling.

Polypropylene carpeting is a popular indoor-outdoor carpeting that is quite durable and easy to keep clean. It can safely be exposed to sparks from a barbecue fire or dropped cigarettes without danger of flaming; but be prepared for melted fibers, which are difficult to camouflage. The disadvantage of this type of carpet is its poor resilience.

Viscose rayon carpets have only a moderate resistance to wear and tear. They soil quickly, but care must be taken not to make them too damp while cleaning. Deal with stains promptly, blotting frequently, and there is a good chance you will succeed in removing them. These carpets are flammable.

Carpet underlay. Some carpets are lined with a heavy foam-rubber backing, which serves as its own underlay. Other carpets need a different form of underlay. There are several gradings of plastic foam, some more spongy than others, and an experienced salesperson will help you choose one that will suit both the type of carpet and its location.

Underfelts made of a mixture of wool, hair, and/or jute are still popular. Some are rubber-coated to make them more mothproof and less likely to absorb spills.

New carpet on an old floor. When old carpet and underlay have been taken up to be replaced by new, heed the following guidelines:

1. Vacuum the room thoroughly.
2. Damp mop the room using a good household cleaner in the water.
3. If a wool carpet is going down, shake powder pesticide around the perimeter of the room, particularly under warped or raised baseboards. If the old carpet was wool and if it appears to have been eaten by moths or carpet beetles, it is wise to have the room pestproofed. Synthetic carpets are not affected by beetles or moths.

Manufacturers usually mothproof woolen carpets before they leave the factory. Check to see if this is the case when purchasing woolen or wool-blend carpets.

CASHMERE

This fabric requires careful hand laundering. Use very cool suds made with a

Carpet Cleaning with Wet Shampoo

If you decide to wet shampoo the carpet yourself, first remove as much furniture as possible from the room. Slip plastic or cardboard discs under the legs of remaining furniture. Lift floor-length curtains out of the way and vacuum thoroughly. Read and follow all instructions. Use only the detergent or cleaner recommended for that particular machine. Provide cross-ventilation by opening doors and windows. After shampooing, smooth pile with a thoroughly clean nylon broom. When the carpet is dry — after several hours, depending on the type of cleaner and method of cleaning used — vacuum slowly and thoroughly to remove the dried detergent.

Never use the carpet until it is dry. Choose good dry weather when you wet shampoo, and let the carpet dry for 15–20 hours before walking on it.

You might find that the carpet pile soils quickly. This can be caused by a buildup of detergent, which attracts grime.

wool-washing detergent. Try to use a sink or tub with a plug so that the water can be released after washing and subsequent rinsings. Cashmere must not be wrung, but it can be spin-dried in your machine. Put a towel or other soft article of clothing into the machine to act as a buffer, or roll the wet garment in a large towel and press out excess water.

Cashmere will stretch with the weight of water, so when wet you should lift it with both hands. Dry inside out, pinned to a sheet hung like a hammock between three or four clotheslines or on a plastic drying rack. If a machine dryer is used, maintain a very low setting. Steam press when dry.

CAST IRON

Kettles soon become corroded with a furrylike deposit on the inside. A "furry" kettle takes longer to boil, but the gritty deposits do not affect the taste of the water.

Treat an iron kettle by filling it with cold water. Add ¼ cup (60 ml) water softener and bring it slowly to a boil. Remove from heat. Let the solution remain until it is cold, then discard. Scrub out the kettle with a nylon brush; rinse out the loosened scale, and rinse again. Repeat if the kettle has been neglected.

A large seashell or smooth stone left in a kettle also helps to loosen the deposits, which are then poured out with the water.

CHILDREN'S CLOTHING

Pre-treat or soak stained items before washing. Many stains will soak out. White and light-colored socks will need pre-soaking. Rub them with soap and soak, or slip them into an enzyme pre-wash solution for half an hour. Then they can be washed in the machine with other clothing.

Woolen and dark socks can be washed in a short cold water cycle with dark shorts and trousers, using a detergent designed for cold water machine washing.

CHINA

To remove brown stains from old china, soak the china in a mild solution of bleach (5 percent) and water. Soak for several hours, then wash and rinse. If the stains return, repeat the process. Stubborn brown stains on old china can be removed with a solution of equal parts vinegar and salt.

Think Prevention
All clothing should be clean before it is stored. Mildew will attack food stains in damp or humid conditions, and the larvae of moths and silverfish can cause irreparable damage to woolens and many other fabrics that have been stored with stains.

CHINTZ

Chintz usually has a permanent glaze but some fabrics are only lightly glazed, and this finish deteriorates when the material is washed. Drycleaning is preferable to maintain the characteristic surface gloss of this fabric.

If the glaze is permanent and the label states that the fabric is washable, do so by hand, not in a machine. Use hand-hot suds and mild detergent. Do not twist or rub the surface. Rinse in cold water and drip-dry until the article is just slightly damp. Iron on the right side with a cool iron.

CHROME

Chrome will rust easily if the surface is eroded by soda, salt, or traces of food. For this reason, use only clean cloths when wiping chromed frames on furniture. Silicone wax can be used, but only on thoroughly clean chrome.

When rust occurs, dip very fine steel wool in the above cleaner and rub gently. Wipe off and spray with a rust inhibitor, available from hardware stores.

Chromium plate can be cleaned with spray-on silicone cream or with automobile polish. Wipe over grease-stained chrome with a cloth wrung out of hot detergent suds containing a few drops of ammonia. Dry well before applying polish.

Do not wipe chromed fittings with a dishcloth. Traces of grease and food will cause deterioration and eventually rust.

Chromium-plated parts of stools, chairs, highchairs, and desks often rust at joints. Rub gently with dry steel wool, and wipe clean with a dry cloth. Apply a thin coat of chrome polish.

CONCRETE OR CEMENT FLOORS

These floors have a tendency to be dusty unless they are sealed with either clear or colored paving paint or cement sealer, both available at paint stores.

Paths, stairs, and outdoor patios of concrete often develop black or green mold during damp weather. To clean them, mix equal parts of household bleach and water. Apply and leave for three minutes. Kill the mold spores by scrubbing the area with a brush or broom.

Treat a small section at a time, then hose off the loosened mold. Be careful outdoors not to run bleach solution into the lawn or flowerbeds.

Spilled milk will leave a greasy mark on concrete. Hose it off with cold water, scrub the stain with hot water containing washing soda — ½ cup (125 ml) to ½ bucketful of water — then hose again.

To remove light oil stains from a cement floor in a garage, saturate half a dozen sheets of newspaper with water and press firmly over the oil stains. Weigh the papers down with bricks or boards. The drying sheets will act as a poultice and absorb most of the oil.

If no fire risk is involved, another method is to sprinkle a little gasoline over the stain and rub in dry cement powder. Cover with a sheet of plastic, leave for two hours, then sweep the cement.

COPPER

Copper pots and pans will buckle if exposed to high heat. Because they will abrade easily, do not use harsh scrapers and cleaners.

To avoid scraping, simply soak the containers with hot detergent suds until the food loosens. Then use a nylon sponge or brush to remove stubborn traces.

Copper can be kept gleaming for a long period of time by using long-term copper polish, now available at most supermarkets.

Blue or green deposits develop quickly on not-quite-clean or not-quite-dry copper surfaces. This is a poisonous deposit, and it should not come into contact with food. The deposit should come off when you rub the item with a cloth dipped in a mixture of vinegar and salt.

Avoid the use of vinegar in any food to be cooked in a copper pan, and remove cooked food as soon as possible from a copper container.

CURTAINS

Many ready-made, lined, synthetic curtains cannot be washed successfully. Although it may be expensive, drycleaning will keep them looking as good as new, whereas washing can cause permanent creasing.

Keep curtains cleaner longer by lightly vacuuming them to remove surface dust. Use the upholstery attachment on the end of the vacuum cleaner hose.

Lace and light synthetic curtains should be taken down, all hooks removed, shaken, then soaked in warm detergent suds for 15 minutes before they are hand-washed. Rinse twice. Drip-dry; the weight of the water will draw out creases. Do not dry these curtains in full sunlight. Rehang as soon as they cease to drip.

Cotton and linen-type curtains may shrink. A curtain rod inserted in the lower hem while the curtains are still slightly damp and rehung in their correct position will help them to drop a little, and its weight will draw out creases. Other curtains will need heavy ironing from top to bottom, not across the fabric.

It is advisable to test the dyes of any colored washable curtains being laundered for the first time. Never use hot water. Pre-soak in cold water with a handful of salt for 15 minutes. Drain that water, then pre-soak for five minutes in mild detergent. Wash in warm water, rinse twice in cold, and immediately hang the curtains to dry.

Long, hanging drapes can be laid across three or four clotheslines to drip-dry. Shorter curtains can be pegged to the clothesline without doubling the material. Others can be hung horizontally.

Worn, threadbare curtains should be handled very carefully. Fold them loosely and slip one (or two small light curtains) into an old pillowcase. Pre-soak the enclosed curtain for 15 minutes, occasionally swirling it in plenty of cool suds. Press out excess soaking water. Wash in the same way and rinse twice. Remove the still-folded curtain or curtains from the pillowcase and roll in a towel. Rehang light synthetic curtains to dry, or dry outdoors and iron if necessary, being careful not to put undue stress upon the worn fabric.

Tears and holes can be mended by dipping a large patch of similar material in raw starch. Lay the patch over the tear, cover it with brown paper, and press hard with a moderately hot iron until the patch adheres. This will last until the curtains are washed again, and the patch will be almost invisible in the hanging folds.

Curtain fittings. One way to brighten rusty metal curtain fittings is to boil them in a vinegar solution —

1 tablespoon (15 ml) to 1 cup (250 ml) water — for 15 minutes. Pat dry without rinsing.

Use plastic curtain fittings if rust is prevalent in a badly ventilated room or in seaside environments.

DENIM AND JEANS

Few denims are fast-dyed; fading often is desirable in this fabric. If soaking is necessary, do so in cool water with an enzyme pre-wash compound; wash in cool suds either by hand or in a machine. Drip-drying makes them slightly stiffer.

Identify Stains

Help your drycleaner by pinning a note to the stains, advising the cleaner of their origin. Be specific rather than general. For instance, if a garment is stained with paint, try to state the brand name and the type of paint, as well as what treatment, if any, you have applied. Do this for all stains — food and drink spills, ink stains, and so on. This will save the cleaner unnecessary experimentation.

Press denim with a hot iron while still slightly damp.

Denim garments that are too stiff to be worn comfortably can be relaxed by adding a fabric softener to the final rinse. Never add fabric softener if suds are present. This treatment can be applied once in three or four washes. Used too frequently, the softener will give the fabric a greasy feeling.

DOWN COMFORTERS

These are best drycleaned, but not every cleaner will accept these heavy items. Careful home laundering is successful in an emergency, either by hand or in a machine, using the shortest cycle on a fully automatic washing machine. Usually a good airing, however, will freshen down or feathers, and the use of a new removable cover will improve the appearance of the comforter. Try to avoid washing.

Feather eiderdowns can tear and the feathers might clog drycleaning equipment or a washing machine, so an assessment of the strength and age of the covering must be made before a feather comforter is machine-washed.

If the corners are worn, reinforce them with corners of contrasting material finely stitched into place before washing the eiderdown.

Machine wash feather eiderdowns for not more than three minutes, interrupting the cycle if necessary. Use the greatest amount of *very cool water* and mild detergent suds. (Hot water will release oils contained in the feathers and cause an unpleasant odor.) Stains on the cover should be pre-treated. A paste made of borax and warm water can be rubbed into old tea and coffee stains. A pre-wash spray can be used on other stains before the cover is wet, or you can dampen the marks and rub in laundry soap. Scrub the stains gently with an old toothbrush.

Rinse for two minutes, interrupting the cycle if necessary, then spin dry. A very low-set electric dryer can be used, provided it is large enough for the eiderdown. Again, heat will cause an unpleasant odor.

If hand washing, use plenty of cool water in a large tub with a plug. Whisk detergent into the water before immersing the quilt. Push it up and down to rinse out dissolved grime. Remove the plug and press out excess water. Rinse twice in the same way. If a spin dryer or wringer is not available, remove further water by rolling the article in a large towel. Hang to dry in a breezy semi-shaded area. If possible, choose a windy day to wash an eiderdown. Use about a dozen clothespins to attach it to the line so that

Redistributing Down

To fluff up a down comforter or jacket, put it in the dryer with a clean tennis ball or a pair of clean canvas shoes. The friction will redistribute the feathers.

it can dry in an even thickness. Turn it several times while it is drying, and loosen clumps of feathers with your fingers.

Washing an old eiderdown might weaken the downproofing of the cover. Spray the surface lightly with spray-on starch or with a silicone-based fabric shield, which will also help to make the cover more grime-resistant.

EMBROIDERED ARTICLES

These should be washed in hand-hot water with mild detergent. Rinse well; starch if necessary. Small articles can be rolled in a towel until it is time to iron them. Use a spray-on starch to restore their stiffness. Iron on the wrong side with the iron heated to suit the material.

New embroidery, which needs freshening after much handling and which is perhaps required for gift-giving or for display purposes, can be dipped in hot water containing 1 tablespoon (15 ml) borax. First ascertain colorfastness. Then push the article up and down in the water. Do not wring or crease. Spread it flat over a towel and cover it with another towel. Press to absorb the water. Then press on the wrong side over a thoroughly clean ironing sheet, using an iron heated to suit the material. Wrong-side pressing raises the embroidery on the right side. Borax will clean and restore a slight stiffness to the material.

To test for colorfastness, use sample threads spread on a white cloth and covered with a wet cloth. Press with a hot iron. If the cloths are stained with dye, do not use hot water; instead use cool water and add to it the borax dissolved in a little boiling water.

FLAMEPROOFED FABRICS

Garments treated with flame retardants should be laundered according to instructions on the label. Do not boil or bleach these garments. As a general rule, wash in cool detergent suds and rinse well to remove traces of the suds.

Note: Flameproof does not mean fireproof. Fabrics will still burn and char, but they will not burst into flame.

FLANNEL

Wash in a machine or by hand. Use cooler water for pajamas and other articles that have been made flame-resistant.

Flannel sheets and pillowcases provide sleeping comfort in cold weather, but the flannel nap can be irritating to people with respiratory problems.

Sometimes flannel poses a dust problem. New sheets have loose nap that sheds fluff and causes furniture to have a dusty appearance, but this problem will ease after several washings.

In the meantime, do not spin dry the sheets. Let them drip-dry. They will be slightly stiffer, but their warmth will not be affected. Shedding will be lessened.

FURNITURE

Wood furniture is usually polished, waxed, lacquered, sealed, or finished in some way — so maintenance is cut to a minimum. Still, regular care and a little knowledge are necessary to keep furniture that is in daily use in good order.

This can be done by keeping it clean and suitably polished. Keep two points in mind:

1. Do not apply polish over a grimy surface. Polish can seal in traces of makeup, food, perspiration, and dirt, causing the surface to become dull and unattractive.
2. Do not use too much polish. A small amount well rubbed in produces far better results than an abundance applied lightly. Test by running your finger over the freshly polished surface; if it leaves a smeared mark the polish has been applied too liberally.

Daily dusting and frequent rubbing with soft cloths will keep polished furniture in excellent condition. As a rule, polish should not be applied every time you rub, unless the furniture has been exposed to heavy use.

Never be afraid to wipe the surface of furniture with a damp cloth to remove surface stickiness. A good cleaning solution for wood furniture can be made by adding 1 tablespoon (15 ml) of vinegar and ½ teaspoonful (2 ml) of liquid detergent to 1 quart (1 liter) of warm water.

Wipe the surface of the furniture methodically, changing the cloth or rinsing it well as it becomes grimy, to prevent redistribution of the dissolved grime.

Immediately follow this treatment with a brisk rub with a dry, soft duster, rubbing in the direction of the wood grain. Then the wood can be polished in the usual way: Spray the duster with polish; do not spray the furniture surface directly. The warmed duster ensures even distribution of the polish.

Silicone spray, again applied on the soft polishing cloth, is also good for highly lacquered finishes.

Surfaces that have always been oiled — teak, for instance — should be maintained with oil.

Do not change or mix polishes. They are often incompatible, and one used on top of another results in dinginess. In the case of waxed antiques, the solvent in another type of polish could reveal pit marks and scars that the original wax had camouflaged.

Extremely grimy furniture can be cleaned with very fine steel wool saturated with raw linseed oil. Rub lightly, wipe off with clean cloths, and polish as usual.

Beeswax polishes. These preserve and enhance solid woods. They are excellent for use on light woods such as pine or oak, where the use of oily polishes would darken the grain. This can be applied to wood, leather, stained wooden surfaces, iron, steel, and bronze. You will need 5 ounces (125 g) beeswax and 1¼ cups (325 ml) turpentine. Melt the beeswax in a pan and remove it from heat.

Carefully stir in the turpentine. (Remember, turpentine is flammable.)

A thicker paste wax is obtained by using less turpentine. A lighter-colored polish can be made by using purified beeswax instead of the yellow.

To make a creamy wax, you will need 3 ounces (75 g) white beeswax, 1 cup (250 ml) turpentine, and 1 cup (250 ml) hot water. Melt the beeswax in a clean pan and remove it from the heat. Stir in the turpentine and then the water. Add ½ teaspoon (5 ml) cloudy ammonia to emulsify the mixture. This wax is excellent for use on inlays and veneers.

Recommendations: Turpentine and kerosene are toxic and flammable. Always use with extreme caution, and store according to hazardous waste regulations. Store in a sealed container.

Availability: Beeswax can be purchased at crafts and health food stores.

Oil-based furniture polishes. These are appropriate for use on dark woods, such as cherry or mahogany. Apply sparingly on a slightly dampened cloth and polish with a dry duster. Oily polishes or raw linseed oil rubbed into the *underside* of antique tabletops "feed" the wood and help to prevent cracking, which can occur in dry climates. Do not use if a synthetic finish has been applied to the wood.

Synthetic furniture finishes. Cellulose and polyurethane finishes are found on many items of furniture. The glossy surfaces are hard and durable. Regular dusting and the occasional application of liquid silicone polish will maintain them well.

If the finish becomes sticky or dull, wipe it over with a sponge cloth wrung out of warm detergent suds containing 1 tablespoon (15 ml) vinegar. Wipe with a second clean damp cloth, then dry and polish in the usual way.

Care must be taken with the use of plastic items on polyurethane surfaces. Plastic reacts with the finish and causes erosion, which will require professional treatment to remedy. Healproof mats should be underlined with cork or felt.

White untreated wood furniture. Scrub with cold water containing household bleach. Rub stains with a cut lemon sprinkled with salt. If that fails, mix equal parts of hydrogen peroxide and cloudy ammonia. Saturate a pad of cotton wool and leave it on the stain for several hours. Rinse well.

Bamboo and cane furniture. Vacuum with brush attachment to remove dust. Wipe over with a damp cloth and polish with silicone wax.

Very dirty and neglected pieces can be scrubbed gently with warm soapy water. If possible, work outside. A hose can be used to rinse off the suds, provided the spray is fine. Dry in indirect sunlight and polish with silicone wax.

The sagging woven cane seat of a chair or stool can be tightened. Work out of doors, and sponge the cane with a salt solution: 1 cup (250 ml) of salt in 1 cup (250 ml) of boiling water. Do not wet surrounding bentwood. Dry outdoors and do not sit in the seat for 24 hours.

Stripping Paint from Wood Surfaces

Follow instructions on the product's label. Work outdoors, over thick pads of newspaper.

High-gloss cellulose finish on solid wood furniture can be removed with a cellulose thinner.

Dark oak can be lightened by removing the stain with paint stripper, following manufacturer's directions. When the oak is dry, sand the surface evenly to remove the remaining stain. Then, treating a small area at a time, rub in warmed linseed oil applied with a soft duster. Repeat 2 or 3 times. Leave for 2 days until the oil is thoroughly absorbed, then polish with white wax or silicone cream.

Hint: It is difficult to successfully remove polyurethane or cellulose high-gloss finish from veneers. Often it is best to avoid lifting and buckling of the veneer by simply painting over the varnish with an attractive antique-type paint finish.

Carved furniture. Carved furniture needs regular maintenance or dust will settle in the grooves. Vacuum regularly, using the brush attachment.

Use a clean paintbrush or old shaving brush dipped in furniture oil or silicone wax to keep carved wood clean and polished.

Drawers. Drawers that do not run smoothly should be examined for loose runners, nails, or screws. Drawers sometimes expand and stick during wet weather, but the wood will shrink again when the atmosphere is drier. In the meantime, rub the runners with candle wax, beeswax, or paste polish to make the drawers operate more smoothly.

Ebony. Wash with a cloth wrung out in vinegar water made of 1 tablespoon (15 ml) vinegar per 2 cups (500 ml) water. Polish with raw linseed oil. This treatment will keep ebony dark and shining.

Enameled furniture. Wipe over with a damp cloth once a week. Occasionally wipe with a cloth wrung out of warm mild detergent suds containing a teaspoonful (5 ml) of borax, or use a soft emulsion-type cleaner on a damp cloth. Remove traces of the suds and cleaner with a second damp cloth. Polish with silicone wax if the paint is dull.

Gilt trimmings. Often found on painted furniture, mirrors, and picture frames, these need regular dusting. If the gilt appears dull, brighten it by rubbing it very gently with a soft cloth sprinkled with mineral spirits. Spray silicone cream onto a clean duster and polish lightly.

Inlaid furniture. This requires careful handling to protect the thin inlays. Polishing cloths should be smooth and unfrayed; loose threads could lift the corners of the inlay. Use a light-colored wax polish rather than oil; the latter will darken lighter inlays and detract from the general appearance.

Leather upholstery enjoys a well-earned reputation for durability unmatched by other upholstery materials. Only minimal maintenance is needed — an occasional wipe with a piece of soft toweling or a sponge cloth wrung out of warm suds made with a wool-washing liquid or powder, or with a smudge of dishwashing soap or glycerin soap on the damp cloth.

Treat about one square yard (meter) at a time and go over the cleaned section with a second cloth wrung out of clear water. This will remove traces of dissolved grime and soap. Create a cross-breeze in the room so the damp leather will dry quickly. Never expose upholstery leather to strong sunlight.

This simple treatment two or three times a year, depending on what use the furniture has had, will keep the upholstery clean and shining.

Marble surfaces. Undiluted liquid detergent applied on a soft cloth will remove light stains from marbled surfaces. To remove other stains, rub with toothpaste, then rinse off. Rub with a cloth moistened with turpentine to restore the polish.

Badly discolored and neglected marble can be brightened by smearing heavily with a paste made of mild scouring powder and crushed washing soda (two parts soda to one part powder). Mix to a paste with boiling water and leave on the marble for 24 hours. Wipe off, then polish with turpentine or silicone wax. *Note:* Protect marble from acids — they will erode the surface.

Wicker furniture. Wickerwork is created by weaving or plaiting water reeds or osiers, and it benefits by being thoroughly wet down from time to time. However, this treatment is limited if wicker is combined with wood. First vacuum, using the brush attachment, to extract surface dust. Scrub with light detergent suds containing one tablespoon (15 ml) borax. Avoid overwetting. Rinse off with a textured cloth, lightly wrung out of clean

Oxalic Acid
This acid is poisonous and must be handled cautiously. Wear gloves.

Thoroughly hose out the bucket used for rinsing. Contact your local hazardous waste authority for proper disposal of the cloths and can that held this mixture.

water containing salt. Dry in a breezy place, out of direct sunlight. When the wicker-work is completely dry, spray with silicone furniture cream. Do not sit on wicker seats until they are completely dry; wet wicker will sag.

Wax stripper, the kind used for removing accumulated wax polish from floors, also can be used to remove wax from old furniture. Test on an inconspicuous section before proceeding.

Oxalic acid is also a good bleach to whiten stripped, stained furniture. Mix in the proportion of 1 ounce (25 g) to a full cup (250 ml) of warm water. Mix the solution in an old can using a stick. Stand the can on several sheets of newspaper as you work. Paint the acid on to the wood and let it dry. Then, still wearing gloves, rinse it off with plenty of cold water containing ½ cup (125 ml) of ammonia, which will neutralize the acid.

FURS

Ideally, any fur garment should be professionally cleaned once a year before it is stored for the summer. Stains caused by cosmetics, drinks, and food spills provide attractive lures for moths, which can ruin a fur.

Furriers will clean and store fur garments if home facilities are inadequate. However, it is not always convenient or economical to store a fur. Storage at home means that the fur is readily accessible. Providing certain guidelines are followed, a fur can be adequately stored at home.

A dull, brittle fur needs professional cleaning, but a lustrous fur with an isolated stain can be treated at home. Lightly sponge a stain on a dark fur with drycleaning fluid.

Rub oven-heated bran (the edible kind, which is cleaner) into a light-colored fur. Work over an old sheet; roll up the fur and leave it for three days before shaking it out of doors and brushing it lightly with a clean clothes brush.

Sponge the lining with drycleaning fluid, particularly around the neckline where cosmetics and perspiration stains are most evident. Avoid overuse of the cleaner. It should not penetrate to the backing.

Store the fur on a well-padded hanger in a bag made of unbleached calico. This bag should be longer than the garment, so that paradichlorobenzene crystals (from a hardware store or drugstore) can be placed in the bottom of the bag where they will not come in contact with the fur. These crystals are an exellent moth deterrent, but they can cause discoloration if they come into direct contact with the fur over a long period. Use about 1 tablespoonful (15 ml) of crystals. Tie the bag firmly around the crook of the hanger.

The fur should be examined every six weeks for moths. Shake it well and air it in the shade, never in the sun. Place fresh crystals in the bag to compensate for evaporation of the original ones. Retie the bag tightly.

GLASS

To clean discolored glass, soak in ammonia and water for several hours. Or, soak in vinegar with the contents of a tea bag, then wash and rinse. Badly discolored glass can be cleaned by soaking it in acetone for a few hours. Follow with a thorough wash and rinse.

To clean glass tabletops, try rubbing them with lemon juice. For scratches in glass tabletops, try rubbing some toothpaste on the scratch

Glass chandeliers. To clean glass chandeliers, wipe the prisms with a soft cloth moistened with commercial window cleaner or with water containing 1 tablespoon (15 ml) ammonia. The use of ammoniated water helps to remove insect marks more easily.

If the prisms merely need dusting, brush them lightly with a feather duster; or slip on a pair of old cotton gloves, dampen them, and wipe over the crystals by hand.

If it is possible to take down the chandelier for cleaning, line a tub or sink with an old towel, and add warm water, detergent, and a tablespoon (15 ml) of ammonia. Wash and rinse carefully. Then spray with silicone wax.

Wipe the light bulbs and check the metal pieces attached to the pendants before rehanging.

HAIRBRUSHES

Brushes are more easily cleaned if two are washed at the same time. Scrub one with the other to clean bases and bristles. Dip in soapy water containing 1 teaspoon (5 ml) ammonia to dissolve grease. Rinse well. Dry brushes on their sides to prevent distortion of the bristles.

Wash combs in the same solution, scrubbing the teeth with a nailbrush.

HANDBAGS

Evening bags. Keep taffeta or satin linings clean by sponging lightly with drycleaning fluid. Air well before closing the bag.

Beaded bags should be treated with care: One broken thread and beads will be lost. Dust white-beaded bags with talcum powder and enclose the bag in a folded towel. Leave it there for 48 hours, then brush lightly to remove the powder.

Leather bags can be sponged with a cloth wrung out of warm water, then lightly rubbed with good quality soap. Wipe off the soapy deposits with two or three clean damp cloths. When the bag is dry, polish with leather polish or cream. Then leave the bag in the sun for half an hour so that the polish will be absorbed and it will not rub off onto clothing.

Brush or vacuum the lining to remove fluff and dust. Sponge soil marks with drycleaning fluid and air well before closing the bag.

Never store a leather handbag on or under a plastic handbag. The plastic bag will absorb dye from the leather bag and it will become permanently stained.

Leather bags might become moldy in wet humid weather, and stored bags should be examined frequently under these adverse climatic conditions.

Mildew can be removed from leather bags, belts, and shoes by wiping or brushing it off outdoors. Wipe the mildewed surface with a damp cloth. When dry, rub in petroleum jelly. Let the vaseline absorb before cleaning in the usual way.

Wipe with a damp cloth to remove light soil marks and perspiration, then spray with silicone wax and rub gently.

Patent leather bags. Buff to a shine with a little petroleum jelly or silicone spray.

Plastic bags. Sponge clean with a damp cloth lightly coated with a good quality household soap. Wipe off the soapy residue with several damp cloths; dry, then spray with silicone wax and buff to a glow.

Suede bags should be brushed frequently using a suede-cleaning brush. Grease marks, often caused by perspiring hands, can be sponged with drycleaning fluid.

Raise the flattened nap by rubbing lightly with fine sandpaper.

A light steaming will also raise a flattened nap. Hold the bag briefly over steam rising from boiling water in a shallow pan — the less water, the more steam. Prolonged steaming might dissolve adhesives. Dry, then use a sponge or a suede brush to raise the nap.

HARDWOOD FLOORS

Hardwood floors, if well sealed, need little maintenance. Common sealants include varnish and polyurethane. For either type, damp mopping will remove grime; dry mopping on a daily basis will get rid of dust and grit that can get ground in and wear away the finish.

In time, even with care, traffic areas will show signs of wear. Touch up these areas with the same type of sealant originally used on the floor. Because some sealants are incompatible, it is not advisable to use one type on top of another. And if a floor has had even one coat of wax, it cannot be sealed successfully unless every trace of wax has been removed, usually accomplished by resanding the entire floor.

Sealant protects the boards from moisture, which can cause warping and coarsen the grain.

Chairs and movable furniture should be fitted with protective plastic glides to avoid damage to the seal.

KITCHEN COUNTERTOPS

Countertops are durable and easy to maintain, but care should be taken not to use them as cutting boards or as a rest for hot pans. Always use a cutting board when slicing anything. If the counter is used as a cutting board even once, microscopic cuts or scratches result that will collect traces of grime. These will dull the sheen of the laminate. Always place some protection under hot pots.

Always use a clean cloth or sponge when wiping the kitchen countertops.

KITCHEN SINK

Enamel and porcelain-enamel sinks are less durable than stainless steel. Enamel will chip easily, so it is advisable to line the bottom of an enamel sink with a plastic or rubber mat when washing up heavy ovenproof dishes and saucepans. An emulsion-type cleaner can be used to remove light stains that do not respond to powdered or liquid detergent. Severe stains will respond to soaking with diluted household bleach or to an application of a paste made by mixing cream of tartar with peroxide.

Fiberglass sinks are attractive, but they scratch easily. Care should be taken when washing cutlery or sharp household items. Keep fiberglass sinks shiny by wiping them with liquid detergent on a damp cloth. Rinse with hot water and wipe dry.

Plastic sinks are not intended for heavy use. They are light and ideal for use in recreational vehicles and small boats. They must be protected from scratches and burns caused by hot pots and dishes and cigarettes. Spilled chemicals will dull the surface, and cracks might be caused by dropped articles, such as cans of food from an above-sink cupboard. To clean plastic sinks, use metal polish.

Stainless steel sinks are very durable for family use and require little maintenance. To remove grease, use liquid detergent on a soft cloth. An emulsion cleaner may be used occasionally to restore the sheen. The use of powdered detergents can cause rainbow effects on stainless steel. If you use a powdered detergent, rinse completely and dry the stainless steel immediately.

LACE

Because of its delicacy, lace should be handled carefully. The weight of water can cause tears. Valuable old lace can be washed in a large jar with a firm-fitting lid. Add mild detergent or soap flakes to warm water in the jar, tighten the lid, and shake until it is well mixed. Then immerse the lace and shake the jar for a minute or so. Rinse in the same way.

If the lace is very frail, tack it to a white cloth before washing it. After washing and rinsing, simply spread out the cloth and the lace to dry.

Never use bleach on old lace. Rain or dew will bleach it naturally. Tack the lace to a towel or sheet and peg the ends between two clotheslines, like a hammock. This will expose the lace to dew or rain in a safe, off-the-ground position.

Wash frail lace curtains inside a pillowcase after folding each one loosely. Thus protected, they can be pushed up and down in mild suds and rinsed in the same way after sudsy water has been pressed out.

Press lace on the wrong side so that the pattern will be raised. Every care should be taken not to dig the point of the iron into the fine threads. Lead with the back or the side of the iron to avoid this possibility.

LAMB'S WOOL

Wash in very cool suds with wool-washing detergent or mild soap flakes. Dry inside out. Sweaters dry best on a plastic drying rack. Or slip the legs of a pair of pantyhose through the sleeves and peg the toes and waist of the pantyhose to the line.

LAMPSHADES

Stitched, fabric-covered lampshades are washable. Swirl them around in tepid detergent suds, rinse under a running tap, pat with a towel to absorb excess water, and dry as quickly as possible.

Shades that are glued must not be wet; the adhesive will not withstand water. Instead, first dust them by brushing with a clean clothes brush, then wipe the shades on both sides with a piece of toweling moistened with drycleaning fluid. Change the position of the cloth frequently to prevent the redistribution of loosened grime.

Scorch marks caused by the heat of a light blub that is too large or too strong for a small shade cannot be removed. The material is weakened by heat, and treatment usually results in damage to the shade.

Parchment shades should be dusted regularly. Occasionally they can be wiped over with a barely damp cloth or rubbed with a slice of fairly fresh bread. Work over newspaper to catch the grimy crumbs as they fall.

Plastic and fiberglass shades can be washed in tepid detergent suds. Rinse well. After drying, rub lightly with a cloth dampened with spray-on silicone wax.

Collapsible balloon or pendant-shaped paper shades must not get wet. Dust them well; then, working over an old sheet, sprinkle them freely with powdered starch or talcum powder. Let the shades collapse, wrap them loosely in the sheet, and leave them for 24 hours. Dust again to remove traces of powder.

LEATHER

Clean leather items or upholstery with a damp cloth and some saddle soap. Prevent leather from cracking by polishing occasionally with a solution of vinegar and linseed oil (1:2).

To remove white water spots from leather, cover the spots with a thick coat of petroleum jelly, and leave it in place for a few days. Wipe with a soft cloth. Petroleum jelly and hairspray will also remove ballpoint ink from leather.

LINED GARMENTS

Follow the manufacturer's label. Many need to be drycleaned because laundering will distort the lining and interlining, causing the garment to lose its shape.

LINEN

Pure linen is a natural fiber made from flax. Many linen fabrics contain blends of synthetic fibers. Soiled garments should be pre-soaked for 10 minutes in warm suds, then washed in hot suds and rinsed twice. Remove pure linen garments from the line or dryer while still slightly damp, and if a sheen is not desirable, press with a hot iron on the wrong side. Press on the right side if a sheen is preferred. Press synthetic linen combinations with a cooler iron; test on an inner seam if you are in doubt. Air well before storing in a closet.

MARBLE

To remove stains and water marks from marble, use a cream-type silver polish. Or scrub with a paste of salt and lemon juice. For persistent stains, treat with hydrogen peroxide and a couple drops of ammonia. Pour the mixture on the stain, wait a few minutes, then wash and rinse the area.

It is important to remember not to rub marble surfaces too hard. Always try nonabrasive cleaners and approaches first. If possible, move the marble item into the sunlight.

Oil-based cleaners or waxes can cause discoloration of marble and should be avoided.

MIRRORS

Make your own cleaning solution for mirrors: Mix 2 tablespoons (30 ml) of vinegar and 5 tablespoons (75 ml) of ammonia in 1 quart (1 liter) of water.

MOHAIR

Hand wash in plenty of very cool suds using a wool-washing detergent or hair shampoo. Rinse twice. Hand-knitted mohair sweaters might stretch with the weight of water in them, so launder them by hand in a tub with a plug. Squeeze and knead to loosen grime. Remove the plug and press out surplus water. Add cold rinsing water and repeat. Avoid allowing the incoming water to hit the garment with force as the tub refills. Finally, roll the garment in a thick towel and press out as much water as possible. Dry flat, inside out, and turn the garment halfway through the drying time. Thick wads of newspaper spread over a clean cement surface or a dry lawn and weighted down can be used to keep drying garments clean and to speed the drying process. When dry, shake lightly to raise the pile.

NETTED MATERIALS

Some mosquito nets act as a magnet to dirt particles, either in the air or in washing water. They tend to become dingy looking unless they are washed frequently and separately.

Shake the net, pre-soak it for 15 minutes in cool detergent suds, then launder it in cool detergent suds. Rinse three times. Dry in the shade. Sunlight will yellow these nets.

Cotton nets can be machine-washed without any problem. Shake, pre-soak, then wash. Carefully pull the net into shape to dry in full sunshine.

Holes in nets can be mended almost invisibly by covering them with a larger patch of net dipped in raw starch, that is, starch made into a thick paste with cold water. Arrange the patch over a hole, cover it with brown paper, and press with a fairly hot iron. Be very careful not to let the iron touch the surrounding net.

NYLON

Nylon has a static electricity effect that attracts dirt and grime particles. If these work into the fiber, restoring the original clean appearance will prove more difficult.

Nylon articles should be laundered after every wear, using warm water and detergent or soap flakes. Wash thoroughly, rinse very well, and drip-dry immediately.

Stains on nylon fabrics should be treated before they set. Drycleaning fluid and spot cleaners can be used on nylon, but liquid bleach must not be used, unless advised on the label.

When nylon is blended with another fiber, for instance with cotton or wool, wash the garment according to the requirements of the weaker fabric. The labels on fabric bolts and on garments will show the percentages of each. If ironing is necessary, use only a low-set iron.

Nylon and nylon-blended fabrics will cling to the body in dry cold weather or in an atmosphere controlled by air conditioning, which reduces the amount of moisture in the air. Static cling can be reduced by adding fabric softener (*not* water softener) to the final rinse once in four or five launderings.

ORGANDY

This is a fine, stiffened fabric usually made of cotton. Wash in plenty of hand-hot water in which mild soap flakes have been well dissolved. Push the garment up and down in the suds but do not scrub or rub. Rinse two or three times. Slip the garment onto a hanger to dry and remove it from the clothesline while still slightly damp. Press at once with a medium-hot iron to restore the garment's crispness, and continue to iron until the organdy is quite dry. An extra natural crispness can be imparted by dipping the nearly dry garment in 4 cups (1 liter) warm water containing 1 tablespoon (15 ml) borax. Then rehang until it is time to iron the garment. Light spray starch can also be applied when ironing.

Some organdy blends scorch easily. Be cautious when ironing.

OVEN

Much has been done to improve stove finishes so that cleaning the stove is not as difficult as it once was. Lift-off oven doors and removable enameled trays fitted to line the floors of the oven and grill have simplified oven cleaning.

There is a growing demand for self-cleaning oven surfaces. These work in two ways:

1. **Pyrolytic cleaning is the process by which the oven is heated to a certain high temperature, which reduces spatters and general oven soil to fine ash. There is a separate control for this cleaning cycle, which takes up to two hours. During this period, the oven door must be kept closed.**

2. **Continuous or catalytic cleaning is carried on with normal cooking temperatures whenever the oven is used.**

For older-type ovens without these built-in cleaners, the use of a commercial cleaner is advised. These are available in spray, paste, liquid, cream, or stick form, and all work in much the same way, dissolving burnt-on grease, which can then be wiped away. The liquid cleaners should be handled carefully, and the area in front of the stove should be protected to avoid ruining the floor. Gloves should be worn when any cleaner is used.

Unless otherwise indicated by the manufacturer, the best time to clean the oven is after cooking, while the oven is still warm. Softened by heat, the grease and soil marks are more easily removed.

Oven cleaning can be minimized if a few general hints are observed:

➤ Meat and foods that have a tendency to spatter should be covered with foil or be enclosed in an oven bag.

➤ Slip a layer of foil or a tray under puddings, casseroles, or pies that might have a tendency to run over and drip.

➤ Always wipe out the oven while it is warm. This also applies to the see-through glass oven door. Dip a damp cloth in a little ammonia to aid in cleaning.

If an oven cleaner is not available, saturate a cloth with ammonia and wipe the sides, floor, and door of the oven. Put about ½ cup (125 ml) ammonia in a saucer with the cloth, and close the door. The ammonia fumes will soften the carbonized grease, and after 8 hours it can be removed by wiping with a soapy steel wool pad. Wipe clean with a damp cloth — traces of soap or detergent also bake on with heat.

Do not use caustic or gritty cleaners on the main outer surface of the stovetop. If there are stains, use an emulsion-type cleaner on a damp cloth.

If the stainless steel trays under the coils on your electric burners are irremovable, lift the coils and pour about a tablespoon (15 ml) of cloudy ammonia into each tray. Leave for an hour or longer. Wearing gloves (and working in a ventilated kitchen), scrub the trays with soapy steel wool, wiping up with paper towels as you work. Wipe the trays with a cloth wrung out in light detergent suds.

This treatment will remove burnt-on deposits. Consider the use of foil liners for these trays. They will save much work.

To clean removable trays, soak them in water with ¼ cup (60 ml) of ammonia. Scrub with steel wool.

OXIDIZED METALS

These are found in old homes, usually as door knobs and drawer and door latches. They should *not* be treated with metal polish. Instead, rub them with a damp cloth and, after a few minutes, with a cloth sprayed with silicone cream, which will offer some protection from rust.

Rusted oxidized metals should be wiped over with a soapy cloth, and then with a clean, damp cloth. Rub in petroleum jelly, machine oil, or olive oil, and let this remain for several hours. Then wipe it off and apply silicone furniture cream.

PAINTED SURFACES

Painted surfaces, in bathrooms and kitchens especially, are subjected to steam and condensation unless a ventilator fan is installed and utilized. An occasional washing of the walls with a commercial paint cleaner helps to restore the gloss and remove traces of grime, which are detrimental to paint.

Walls should be washed from the floor level, working upward. If you start at the top, rivulets of water run toward the floor. These drips, charged with cleaner, act as grime looseners on their way down. They are difficult to remove and stand out in contrast to the areas that have been wiped over.

Start at the bottom and working up, cover about a square yard (meter) at a time. Work with two buckets, one containing the cleaning solution, the other containing clean, warm water and a sponge. Change the rinse water frequently.

PARQUET FLOORS

These attractive wood-block floors should never be exposed to unnecessary wetting. Water or spills can cause the wooden blocks to swell and become uneven. Sometimes sanding is necessary to restore the level of the floor.

Parquet floors can be sealed or waxed. Modern seals make the blocks less vulnerable to wetness; they enhance the beauty of the grain and provide a strong, durable finish that requires only daily dry mopping to remove dust. Damp mop occasionally to clean.

The seals wear well and can be replaced in the traffic areas as they wear, usually after some years.

If the blocks have been waxed, sanding will be necessary before a seal can be applied.

If wax polish is used, apply it in time to let it dry, then buff with a polishing machine. The surface will be harder and more brilliant, and it will last longer.

Furniture legs should be protected with plastic glides or with rubber tips to prevent scratching.

PATENT LEATHER

Wipe patent leather with a cloth dampened with vinegar. Then wipe dry with a clean, soft cloth.

PEWTER

Modern pewter contains a high percentage of tin, and it is more tarnish-resistant than antique pewter. It requires little maintenance except for regular dusting with a soft duster.

Pewter comes in two finishes, one with a clear high sheen resembling silver and the second with a satin finish to give an antique appearance. After use, wash both kinds in hot suds, rinse in warm water, and buff with a soft cloth.

Acids will stain pewter, so avoid using pewter bowls for salads containing lemon or any other citrus juice, vinegar, pickles, sauces, or condiments unless the bowl has a liner or unless the containers or pewter servers can be washed without delay. A liner of foil can sometimes be used to protect the finish.

Some pewter flatware cannot be cleaned in a dishwasher. Check with the retailer when making a new purchase of pewter to be sure about this.

The use of pewter or silver polish will remove light scratching to which this soft metal is susceptible, and it will restore the appearance of articles that have been exposed to sea air.

PILLOWS

Fiber-filled pillows tend to flatten with use. Bounce, bulk, and softness can be restored by washing them every couple months, choosing a windy day. In an automatic machine, using the shortest cycle, these pillows can be washed in cold or lukewarm water with mild detergent suds, rinsed, and spun dry. If washing by hand, use cool suds and press out the surplus water. Rinse twice, then press and roll out as much water as possible. Hang to dry in a semi-shaded breezy position, turning frequently. If water in the casing takes a long time to drip, prick the casing with a darning needle in several places.

Placing the pillow in a dryer turned to its lowest setting will also fluff the flattened filling.

Feather pillows also require very cool sudsing and shade drying. Heat can release traces of oil in the feathers and cause them to smell. If the featherproofed cover is very soiled, it is advisable to undo it a few inches (centimeters) and to shake out the feathers into a clean casing or into a large paper bag until the original cover can be soaked and washed. Sometimes pillows become badly stained by medicines, beverages, and so on, and specific washing of the casing is necessary. Treat the stains according to their nature; pre-soak, then wash in hand-hot suds.

Other fillings in pillows should be washed according to the manufacturer's instructions.

PLUSH

Used for upholstery and curtains, plush can be made of silk, of synthetic fibers, or of rayon. Silk and rayon plushes are best drycleaned. Synthetic plush fabrics and fake fur should be treated according to the manufacturer's label.

Plush-covered toys. Some soft toys can be washed in a machine; others must be hand-washed, and still others should be shampooed or drycleaned. Follow instructions on the label; these will depend on the type of filling in the toy.

For toys that can be shampooed, first shake or vacuum to remove surface dust. Dampen the plush evenly, then rub in a small amount of shampoo or mild detergent. Gently scrub the nap, then remove the suds with a series of clean damp cloths. Hang to dry in a breezy position or dry in a low-set dryer. Before and during the drying process, smooth the pile with a clean clothes brush.

POLYESTER

This fiber is used extensively in garments. Hand wash in hand-hot water; machine wash in warm or cold water to minimize wrinkling. Try to wash in a load of similarly colored garments and those of a similar fabric. Wash before the garments are badly soiled; some soil stains are difficult to remove. Hang to dry out of direct sunlight. Except for slacks, shorts, and trousers, try to hang the garments (using plastic-coated hangers) that are not being worn.

POLYURETHANE

Polyurethane fibers have now replaced rubber for making elasticized swimwear, brassieres, foundation garments, support stockings, stretch tights, and shorts. Polyurethane is also used for fillings and paddings.

Wash **elasticized garments** in hand-hot water with detergent, or machine wash using a short cycle and warm water. Dry in semi-shade, not in direct sunlight. Do not expose to high temperature in a dryer.

POPLIN

Once this was made of 100 percent cotton, but now it can be made of wool, silk, or rayon. It should be washed according to the composition of the fiber.

Cotton poplin, often used for shirts and blouses, can be washed in hot water. Dry dyed cotton poplin garments inside out; lightly starch or spray with liquid starch when ironing.

Silk and rayon blends require hand washing in mild warm suds. Roll wet garments in dry towels or dry garments in wet towels and iron when a uniform dampness is obtained. Or, test an inside facing to see if steam ironing is sufficient to remove wrinkles.

Wool poplin can be drycleaned or carefully hand-washed in cool, mild suds. Roll in a towel to absorb surplus moisture, dry inside out on a well-padded hanger, then steam press.

Silk poplin, like some silks, may lose its luster after it has been laundered. This can be restored by rinsing the clean damp garment in vinegar water using 2 teaspoons (10 ml) of white vinegar to one quart (liter) of cold water before drying. If this acid rinse is used, soak the garment in clean, cold water for 30 minutes before it is laundered again. Iron while slightly damp.

PORCELAIN

For dark marks on porcelain, mix a paste of hydrogen peroxide and a scratchless cleanser. Add to this mixture ⅛ teaspoon (1 ml) of cream of tartar. Cover the stains with this mixture and let the porcelain stand for half an hour. Rub with a sponge, then rinse.

To remove the green stains on porcelain left by copper piping, combine equal parts of scratchless cleanser and cream of tartar, then add hydrogen peroxide to make a paste. Apply to the stained area and let stand half an hour. Rinse.

QUILTED FABRICS

Hand wash delicate quilted garments. Use plenty of water of a temperature suitable for the fabric involved and mild detergent suds. Do not wring or twist. Remove spots by rubbing in detergent and scrubbing gently with a soft-bristled brush. Rinse well, press out excess water, roll in a towel to absorb still more moisture, then hang in a breezy place to dry, or dry at low temperature in a dryer.

If washing in a machine, use the shortest cycle and cool, mild suds. Rinse and spin dry. If one or two fluffy

Caution

Mildew spores will develop if a damp garment is left rolled up for too long. If there is to be a delay before ironing, put the garment into a plastic bag in the refrigerator or freezer. Mildew spores will not develop in low temperatures.

towels are put in the same load (space permitting), they will act as buffers and protect the padded fabrics.

Dry jackets and robes on well-padded hangers, using old stockings to bolster the shoulder line. Distribute the weight of a bedspread over two or three clotheslines, and halfway through the drying period turn the spread. You also can put it into a dryer with a very low setting to fluff up the padding.

RAINCOATS

Soiled nylon and plastic raincoats can be washed in warm detergent suds. Rinse thoroughly and drip-dry on a plastic hanger.

Remove mud marks on nylon coats by spreading the soiled area on a flat surface and gently scrubbing with a nailbrush.

RAYON

These fibers can be woven to simulate such fibers as linen, wool, silk, and cotton. However, rayon is not as strong as these fibers, and it is noticeably weaker when wet. Care should be taken not to wring, twist, or scrub wet rayon. Wash rayon garments frequently to make hard washing unnecessary.

Rayon invariably requires ironing, and this should be done while the garment is slightly and evenly damp: Roll the dry garment in the folds of a damp towel. After half an hour, when the garment is evenly damp, iron it using the rayon setting on the iron — a moderately hot setting. Air the garment before putting it away.

Iron glossy rayons on the right side and dull rayons on the reverse side.

REFRIGERATOR

Once a week, wash the refrigerator, vegetable crispers, and meat storage bins in cool detergent suds; rinse and dry well. Wipe the interior of the refrigerator with a cloth wrung out of a baking soda solution, one rounded tablespoon (15 ml) to 1 quart (liter) warm water. This is an effective cleaner that leaves no odor. Odors will develop if food is left uncovered or if it becomes bad. Wash out the interior as suggested, and place 1 tablespoon (15 ml) pure vanilla extract in a saucer on a middle shelf. Leave it there for 48 hours.

Tuck an open box of baking soda on a shelf in the back of the refrigerator where it cannot be spilled. The baking soda will absorb food odors. Change the box every four to six weeks. Pour the old box down sink or tub drains to keep them sweet-smelling. Dissolve by running warm water from the tap.

Charcoal is a cheap and effective odor absorber. Dampen a sizable lump and keep it in the egg compartment where it will not mark other foods. It helps to keep the refrigerator sweet-smelling. Hardware stores stock "odor-eaters," which are also effective.

In damp or humid weather, the outside of the refrigerator might "sweat." Wipe it frequently, using a clean, dry towel. Mold will quickly develop where there are traces of food or grime.

To clean black mold from rubber and plastic gaskets around the doors, use 3 parts cold water to 1 part household bleach. Pull a thin cloth dipped in the solution over an ice pick and run it down the pleats and grooves in the door seals. Be careful not to puncture the gaskets. Change the position of the cloth frequently. Alternatively, use an old sterilized toothbrush as a scrubbing tool.

SATEEN

Known as "poor man's satin," sateen can be made of pure cotton, rayon, or a blend of silk and cotton.

100 percent cotton sateen can be treated as any cotton. Use hot water and detergent or soap suds, rinse and dry. Iron on the wrong side first with a light spray of liquid starch, then lightly on the right side to restore the sheen.

Silk-cotton sateen and rayon sateen should be washed by hand in lukewarm water with mild detergent or soap flakes. Rinse twice, and strip, rather than wring, out excess water. Press with a moderately hot iron while still slightly damp, or drip-dry.

SATIN

This material is now available in several fibers, and the manufacturer's instructions should be observed.

Silk satin is often made into underwear. Wash silk underwear by hand in mild soap and very cold water.

Satin made with acetate is practically crease-resistant. It should be washed before becoming badly soiled; use warm water and liquid detergent or mild soap flakes. Do not wring or twist. Push the garment up and down in the water until soiling dissolves. Rinse twice and drip-dry until almost dry, then iron immediately or roll the wet garment in a towel until it is evenly damp and can be ironed.

Crepe satin has a sheen on one side and a crepe backing, and often both finishes are combined in garment making. Wash as above. While there is still a slight dampness in the garment, press with a slightly hotter iron, using long sweeps. (Slower, more deliberate strokes with the iron will leave impressions in the fabric.) If in doubt about which temperature to use, test the heat of the iron on an inside facing or seam. Drycleaning is advisable.

SHEEPSKIN

Coats, rugs, car seats, and so on can be drycleaned to perfection by any cleaner skilled in cleaning animal skins.

If cleaning at home is desirable and the fleece is not badly soiled, try using a carpet-cleaning powder; sprinkle it into the fleece and work it in well with your fingers. Be generous with the powder, which absorbs grime and grease. Roll up the article and slip it into a plastic bag. Leave it for at least 12 hours before shaking or vacuuming to remove the powder. Brush or comb the fleece and shake again before returning the article to use.

Some articles with treated backings can be washed. Follow the manufacturer's instructions carefully. Never use hot water and try to choose a windy day so that the article will dry quickly. If using an electric dryer, set it at the lowest possible temperature.

SHIRTS

Empty the pockets. Treat stains, if any. Rub soiled areas such as the collar band and cuffs with dampened laundry soap or treat them while they are dry with a pre-wash stain loosener. Hand wash in cool detergent suds and rinse well before drip-drying in the shade; or machine wash in the shortest cycle of an automatic machine, using cold or warm water and mild detergent suds.

When washing wash-and-wear shirts, for best results wash in a single shirts-only load, using cool suds and ample water. This gives the garments plenty of room and prevents undue creasing and wrinkling. Remove the shirts from the machine as soon as the cycle is completed and hang them at once to dry. Shirts can be tumble dried in a dryer if a low temperature setting is used, but they should be removed and hung immediately when the cycle is completed. Little or no ironing will be required.

SHOES

Never dry wet shoes in an oven or near direct heat. Synthetic soles and uppers will become distorted and shrunken; leather shoes will shrink and crack.

Wipe mud from wet shoes and apply a coating of matching shoe polish to the damp uppers. Then stuff the shoes firmly with newspaper, pushing it compactly into the toes with the handle of a wooden spoon. This blocks the shoes into shape, and the paper will absorb some of the dampness.

For faster drying, place a low-set hair dryer or an electric fan near the damp shoes. Do not use a radiator. When the shoes are dry, buff them to a shine.

Dyeing shoes. The only shoes that cannot be dyed successfully are made of smooth plastic or nonporous synthetic materials. Most other shoes can be dyed to extend their life, freshen their appearance, or match a special outfit. Shoes in good condition dye best; those with creasing caused by wear will begin to crack in the creases after a short time, yet the work involved in dyeing these shoes might be justified if it saves the cost of new ones.

Apply the dye with light strokes and try not to overlap applications. Let the first coat dry, then give the shoes another application. Several coats deepen the color. Each coat should be light — heavy applications tend to crack.

If matching shoes to a specific color, test one small area first and allow it to dry. Colors lighten when dry.

Masking tape can be used to cover sole and heel edges and the inside of shoes. Wear rubber gloves and work over newspaper to avoid staining skin and countertops.

Fabric shoes. Canvas, denim, satin, and brocade shoes can be protected against bad soil marks by spraying them when they are new with a fabric protector. This will make them water-repellent and less likely to stain. Reapplications will be necessary if canvas and denim shoes are washed.

Brush fabric shoes after each use. An old toothbrush can be kept for this purpose. It is stiff enough to treat fabrics and it can be washed and dried easily.

Use a matching felt pen to touch up scuff marks on the heels of good shoes grated by gravel or worn while driving a car.

Patent leather. Clean with neutral creams, silicone sprays, or a smear of petroleum jelly to restore the shine. Rub well with a soft cloth.

Do not let heels wear down to the heel coverings before having them repaired.

Storing out-of-season shoes and boots. Polish or clean shoes in the usual way and make sure they are quite dry before they are stored.

Vinyl footwear can be stored in plastic bags, but leather and suede footwear should be wrapped in soft cloths or tissue paper. Leather will dry out if stored in plastic.

Ideally, shoes should be blocked with paper or shoe trees. Stuff the shafts of boots with paper.

Make a point of inspecting stored footwear (and belts, bags, and travel goods) for mold in damp and humid weather.

Fleecy, wool- and fur-lined slippers and boots. Clean before they are stored during the summer months. Insert the hose end of a vacuum cleaner inside the footwear and vacuum well. Then dust the lining with carpet-cleaning powder, talcum powder, or powdered starch and let this remain for 24 hours before vacuuming again. This treatment will absorb grease and perspiration and will freshen the linings.

> **Suggestion**
> Turpentine will soften dried shoe polish. Pour 1 to 3 teaspoons (5 to 15 ml) over the caked polish and leave the container in strong sunlight until it softens. Stir with a twig, mixing in more turpentine if necessary.

Protect these linings from moths and silverfish by slipping a few paradichlorobenzene crystals into each shoe before storing. Wrap as suggested above.

Suede shoes and boots. Brush the footwear thoroughly to remove dust before applying suede cleaners, which are readily available in several shades. Use according to directions. Light stains can be erased and flattened nap raised by rubbing the suede gently with fine steel wool or sandpaper. Suede footwear can be renovated by a drycleaner who specializes in the cleaning of skin garments.

Old suede shoes with flattened nap can be rejuvenated by polishing. Stuff the shoes with paper or insert shoe trees, and rub in matching paste polish. Let this dry in the sun and then apply two or three more coats, letting each dry, before finally buffing to a shine.

To treat stains on suede, use an art gum eraser. Small spots on suede can be rubbed with a nail file.

Rubber boots. Wipe or hose off dirt and mud each time the boots are worn. Do not apply shoe polishes of any kind. To store, stuff balls of newspaper in the toes and shaft of each boot so that they maintain their shape. Stand in a paper grocery bag and place in a cool cupboard.

Wet rubber boots will dry quickly if a low-set hair dryer is trained inside each boot. Alternatively, stuff the boots with old towels or balls of newspaper to absorb the dampness.

SILK

Pure silk or fabrics with silken blends should be washed in warm water and mild liquid detergent or soap flakes. Care must be taken not to apply stress by rubbing, twisting, or wringing. Gently squeeze the garment in the suds. Rinse three or four times to remove all traces of soap or detergent.

If washing removes the natural sheen from a silk garment, simply rinse it in cold water containing 2 teaspoons (10 ml) white vinegar. This acid must be soaked out before the garment is washed the next time. Use cold water in a nonmetal container, and soak for 30 minutes.

Restore slight stiffness to silk by misting the surface with liquid spray-on starch while ironing. Hold the pump upright at a greater distance than is usually required and spray very lightly.

SILVER

Silver is a metal that enhances any setting. Its appearance improves with use and its maintenance is made easy with readily available polishes.

There are several excellent silver cleaners on the market. Long-term silver cleaners and foams save much work. Silver dips should be used with caution. If silver plating is wearing thin and the base metal is exposed, the use of silver dip will cause dark stains. These can be removed by repeated applications of silver polish.

Silver cutlery soon becomes stained with egg, salt, vinegar, and condiments. Intensive cleaning can be avoided if silver cutlery is immersed in hot water containing a little liquid detergent as soon as it is cleared from the table.

Restauranteurs find they need to have their plated cutlery replated more frequently since the advent of commercial dishwashers. Electroplaters, the people who restore worn silverware to its pristine beauty, are unanimous in their belief that dishwashing detergents cause the erosion of the plate more quickly than does everyday use and subsequent manual washing in milder suds.

Tarnish marks on egg spoons and on the tips of fork tines can be removed quickly by placing them in an old aluminum saucepan with sufficient cold water to cover the tarnish marks. Add 1 teaspoon (5 ml) baking soda per 2 cups (500 ml) water. Bring to simmering point for a few minutes, then rub with a silver polishing cloth to restore the shine.

Larger neglected and badly tarnished articles or silver articles with ornamentation can be enclosed in crumpled foil and boiled in the same way with baking soda in an aluminum saucepan. This method of tarnish removal subjects the silver plating to less wear and tear than does sustained rubbing. The treatment will dull the silver a little, but this can be restored by rubbing lightly with a soft cloth and silver polish.

Silversmiths, usually listed in the Yellow Pages under "Electroplating," or simply "Plating," can perform miracles with dented and worn sterling or plated articles. The cost is well justified, particularly in the case of worn cutlery and teapots.

Care should be taken with **silver-plated saltshakers** during wet or humid weather. Salt will quickly erode the plating and the base metal. Make a habit of removing salt from a silver shaker that is not in regular use. Wash and dry the shaker thoroughly.

Bluish-green deposits around the shaker hole or above the glass liner of a silver or silver-plated saltshaker are a sign of corrosion. Remove the deposit as soon as possible by repeated rubbing with silver polish. A smear of olive oil over the area will protect it until the shaker is used again. Remove the oil before use.

Silver coffee- and teapots and lidded jugs should not be stored with the lids closed. Frequently a musty smell will develop, and this is difficult to remove.

An End to Tarnish

Silver cutlery will not tarnish during long storage if it is thoroughly dried and wrapped in sets in aluminum foil. Store in a cardboard box or wrap in a cloth and keep the cutlery in a dry place. Dampness and humidity cause tarnish.

You can keep a lump of sugar in an unused, stored tea- or coffeepot to prevent mustiness, but in some climates the sugar will attract pests such as ants and cockroaches. If the pot has been dried thoroughly and the lid is left open, mustiness will not develop.

A deposit of tannin in a silver teapot can be removed with a commercial tannin dissolver or with borax, using 1 rounded teaspoonful (5 ml) to 1 quart (liter) boiling water in the pot. Let the solution stand until it cools, then discard the water and scrub the inside of the pot with a nylon brush. Use pipe cleaners or a fine bottle brush to clean the spout. If the drain holes are badly corroded with tannin, work from the inside and force the pipe cleaner up the spout. Rinse several times.

Embossed and ornamented silver pieces benefit from an application of silver polish. To remove all traces of polish, rub with a cloth dampened with ammonia. The use of an old shaving brush helps to work polish into ornamentation. Rinse in hot suds, then in clear hot water. Dry and buff.

Not all mold spots can be removed. Once silver plating has eroded, the damage is done and replating is the only solution. Some spots will respond to rubbing with ammonia applied on a soft cloth. Another possibility is to make a paste of baking soda and warm water and to rub it into the spots with a strip of uncrumpled aluminum foil. *Note:* Crumpled foil can scratch the soft silver surfaces.

A silver-polishing cloth is useful for the quick maintenance of silver in daily use. Discount and department stores stock these, or they can be made at home.

Use an old soft dish towel or a hemmed square of old flannel dipped in a silver-cleaning solution. Dry and store the cloth in a plastic bag; use it to rub silver after it is washed. Afterwards, rewash the silver if it will be in contact with food. The cloth can be washed regularly and redipped.

SLIPCOVERS

Most slipcovers made of linen or cotton can be washed at home. However, before washing them for the first time, multicolored materials should be tested to see if the dye is fast, particularly if the background is light.

To test for colorfastness, spread a section over the ironing board and cover it with a wet white cloth. Press with a hot iron. If the white cloth is stained with dye, have the covers drycleaned.

Having removed the covers, shake them well to remove surface dust and fluff.

Remove grease spots by spreading them over a padded towel and sponging the area with drycleaning fluid. Work outdoors and away from flame.

Wash one cover at a time. Pre-soak it in tepid detergent suds for 10 minutes. Drain that water and wash in equally cool suds, gently scrubbing the soiled arms and headrests with a soft nailbrush. If that water is very dirty, wash yet again before rinsing twice. Add half a cupful (125 ml) of vinegar to the final rinsing water to brighten fading colors.

Hang in a single thickness, as far as possible out of direct sunlight. Remove the covers from the line while they are still slightly damp.

Press with a moderately hot iron, paying particular attention to pleats. The use of spray starch will give a better appearance.

Place the covers back on the furniture while they are slightly damp. They will more readily stretch when damp; as they dry they will shrink slightly and draw out creases. When they are quite dry, an application of a fabric protector will help to make the freshly washed covers more grime resistant. Be cautious about washing loose covers in a washing machine; the pipings can abrade and come undone with the action of the machine.

STAINLESS STEEL

Stainless steel has proved to be a most practical metal for household use. It is used extensively for cookware, flatware (cutlery), and tableware, as well as for sinks and countertops, basins, tubs, and furniture. It is durable, attractive, and easy to maintain. Stains from the few foods that do spot stainless steel — egg, citrus fruits, salt, and mayonnaise, for example — are easily removed by light rubbing with an emulsion-type cleaner.

When choosing stainless steel articles for table use, look for those with a whiter color. These contain more nickel and will retain their new look longer. Stainless steel with a blue tinge contains more chromium; it is less expensive, though still quite durable.

Sinks, tubs, and sink boards should be wiped dry after each use. An emulsion-type cleaner will remove most stains and is less abrasive than powder cleaners.

Note: Never let silver dip come into contact with stainless steel as the stain will be very difficult to remove.

Stainless steel saucepans might assume rainbow hues if they are exposed to great heat. It is important to watch the saucepan until the contents come to the boiling point, then reduce the heat. Stainless steel retains heat and cooks perfectly at the lower temperature.

Simply pre-soak cooked-on food in a stainless steel pot or pan; the food will lift off easily with a rubber spatula. Never use harsh pot scrubbers to clean stainless steel cookware, just soak them a little longer in hot detergent suds.

A stainless steel cleaner that will erase heat marks is available on the market.

White water spots might form inside pots and pans that have been imperfectly wiped, then stored with the lids on. For best results rinse a hand-washed pot in hot water and dry it while it is still warm.

Caution

Never use steel wool on stainless steel. Instead, rub hard with a sponge or cloth and liquid detergent.

To remove grease, use liquid detergent on a soft cloth. You may use an emulsion cleaner occasionally to restore the sheen. The use of powdered detergents can cause rainbow effects on stainless steel. If one must be used, rinse completely and dry the stainless steel thoroughly and immediately.

Protect stainless steel draining boards with several thicknesses of newspaper if handling undiluted chemicals and bleaches and particularly liquid silver cleaner, which will definitely cause a stain.

STEEL

Steel articles, such as fire tongs and pokers, some barbecue tools, frames of garden furniture, and so on, rust quickly. Rub household goods with fine, dry steel wool to remove rust, then apply rust inhibitor or rust converter (available in hardware stores) according to the manufacturer's instructions.

SUEDE. *See under Shoes*

SWIMWEAR

Swimwear is expensive; correct washing and storage over the winter months will ensure a longer life. It is important to read the label attached to new swimwear and to follow instructions for rinsing and washing designed to suit that particular fabric.

Before storing, if the suit has been worn in chlorinated pool water, soak it for 10 minutes in cold water containing a little water softener. Rinse in cold water, then in cold liquid detergent suds. Rinse well and dry in the shade.

If the suit has been used in saltwater, soak it for a few minutes in cold water to remove traces of salt. Rinse, then launder as suggested above.

Finally, fold the suit in shape and store it in tissue paper or a perforated plastic bag.

Keeping Swimwear Stain-Free

Suntan oils, sunscreens, and cosmetics often cause stains. Light rubbing with liquid detergent will usually loosen them, and they can be rinsed out under a hard-running cold water tap.

TAFFETA

The taffeta effect is now produced in so many fibers that often it is simpler to have the article drycleaned rather than experiment with laundering methods at home. The attractive stiffness of taffeta can be lost through mishandling.

Acetate and rayon taffetas are often made into bedspreads, curtains, and cushion covers. Hand wash them, using as much water as possible so that the folds are suspended in water and the taffeta will not crush. Push the article up and down in the water to rinse out suspended grime.

It is generally convenient to wash these articles in a tub so that after washing and rinsing the old water can be drained and fresh water run in.

Drip-dry taffetas to retain extra stiffness. Try to avoid the mark of clotheslines on large articles such as bedspreads. This can be achieved by first laying a sheet over three or four parallel lines, then placing the spread over the sheet. Alternatively, you may peg the borders of the spread between three or four lines.

Nylon taffetas should be hand-washed in warm water with liquid detergent suds. Rinse twice and drip-dry. Under this category of taffeta comes stiffened taffeta which is used for half slips and linings for

Ironing Taffeta

Iron taffeta while still slightly damp. A light misting of liquid starch held at a distance (so that concentrated spray will not cause blotching) will help to restore lost crispness.

garments that require light, stiff bolstering.

Stiffened taffetas must not be overhandled. Treat dirty hemlines with pre-wash spot cleaner before washing while the fabric is dry. Then spread the hemline onto a flat surface, and using a soft natural-bristled nailbrush, gently scrub the grime marks.

Use equal parts of warm water and liquid detergent to do this. Then push the garment up and down in plenty of lukewarm water with mild detergent or soap suds. Rinse twice or hang it by the waist with clothespins and lightly hose away the suds. This way, the original stiffness will be retained. If ironing is necessary, press lightly just before it is completely dry using a low-set iron.

TIES

Expensive silk ties are best drycleaned, but they can be cleaned at home using drycleaning fluid poured into a basin. This fluid is flammable, so work in a well-ventilated place away from fire or flame.

Use an old clean toothbrush to gently scrub stains. Move the ties freely in the fluid to remove grime and dirt. Wearing gloves, strip out excess fluid with your fingers, and air the tie in the shade in a breezy place.

Most ties are now lined with a washable fabric, and with care they will retain their shape. Do not twist or wring. Hand wash in lukewarm detergent suds, removing spots with an old toothbrush. Rinse well and drip-dry by hanging them over a clothesline. Finger smooth while they are still wet. If ironing is necessary, first pull the tie into shape, using long tacking threads if necessary, then steam press on the wrong side.

Wool-woven ties usually need tacking along the sides and across the wider end to maintain their shape while they are being washed.

TIN

Some kitchen tools and gadgets are made of tin, which will rust easily if the

Treating New Tinware
New tinware can be treated to make it more rust-resistant. Rub lard or unsalted fat evenly onto the surfaces and bake the article in a slow oven for 15 minutes.

articles are not properly dried or if they are stored under damp or humid conditions. Dry them in sunshine or in a warm oven before storing. Remove light rust marks by rubbing with dry steel wool. Wash in hot suds, then rinse in hot water and dry well.

Aluminum has replaced most tin in baking sheets, cake pans, and so on. Tin has its disadvantages — it rusts if not properly dried, and it darkens with heat and use. While this darkening detracts from its appearance, many excellent cooks and bakers believe that such utensils cook more evenly.

Wash tin articles in hot suds, rinse thoroughly, and dry well in bright sunlight or in a warm oven. To remove burnt-on stains, after soaking in deep suds containing washing soda, rub the surface with well-soaped steel wool.

TOWELS

Dark-dyed towels are not as absorbent as light-colored towels. It is possible that there will be dye loss during the first wash or two, so avoid dye marks on lighter articles by washing new towels alone.

Very grimy towels should be pre-soaked or put through the pre-wash cycle of the machine.

Fabric softener can be used to give softness and fluffiness to towels. This should be added to the final rinse water. Do not overuse — once in three or four washes is adequate. If softener is used too frequently, towels will feel slippery and become less absorbent.

Absorbency. Purchasers of some shear or cropped-pile towels complain that despite a thick pile and close weave, these towels do not absorb well. The pile is too smooth, chilly to the touch, and has a slinky feel that is unpleasant. More absorbent towels have a looped pile. Although all new towels should be washed before they are used to remove the sizing and make them more absorbent, washing has no effect on close-weaved, thick-piled towels. Here are some tips on how to make these towels more absorbent:

➤ Soak them for 12 hours in plenty of cold water with 2 tablespoons (30 ml) Epsom salts, moving frequently. Wring and wash as usual in the machine, preferably using a cold water detergent.

➤ Do not spin dry. After the rinse cycle, remove the towels from the machine and drip-dry on the line. This treatment will result in a coarser, more absorbent finish.

➤ Use and wash the towels as often as possible, following these instructions. It could take up to a dozen launderings for the towels to become more absorbent.

➤ Do not use fabric softener and do not put them in a dryer.

➤ It also helps to hang these towels in heavy rain, allowing them to dry on the clothesline as the weather improves.

TRIACETATE

This is labeled Arnel, Trilan, or Tricel. Wash in luke-warm suds made with mild soap flakes or liquid detergent. Rinse well and drip-dry.

Many triacetates can be machine-washed, but check the label inside the garment to make sure. Wash in the shortest cycle using cold or lukewarm water; rinse and either spin dry or drip-dry. Remove garments from the machine as soon as the cycle is completed to avoid unnecessary creasing. Ironing should not be necessary, but if a touch-up is required, do so with care using a low-set steam iron when the article is dry.

TRICOT

Read the label and wash according to the fiber used—nylon or viscose rayon.

TULLE

Tulle is now made from a variety of fibers, and washing instructions depend on whether this fine net is basically made of nylon, rayon, or cotton. Tulle soon loses its attractive stiffness. Sometimes this can be restored by ironing it while it is still damp, using a medium-hot iron. Always test a small section first. Some tulle shrivels with heat and completely disintegrates.

To avoid digging the point of the iron into this frail fabric, work over a lightly padded board, which will provide a harder base, or lead with the side or the back of the iron rather than with the point.

Tulle edges might appear bedraggled after washing. Trim these with scissors to improve their appearance.

TWEED

Tweed made of pure wool should be drycleaned. Even blended tweeds look better if they have been drycleaned and steam-pressed. If drycleaning costs are not justified for an old garment, wash it in lukewarm suds using a wool-washing detergent or mild soap flakes. Rinse twice. Spin dry, if possible, or roll in a towel to extract surplus water, then dry quickly in a breezy place. Steam press.

UMBRELLAS

To clean pastel-colored nylon umbrellas that have been soiled with grime and mud, work outdoors. Open the umbrella and sponge it all over with drycleaning fluid. Use a series of clean cloths and discard each as it becomes soiled.

Next, prepare a bowl of warm soapy water. Scrub the nylon gently with a soft nailbrush. Hose inside and out to remove all traces of suds.

Wipe the inside frames with an old towel and dry the umbrella in its open position without delay. Never store a closed damp umbrella as its framework will rust.

Black umbrellas look fresher if they are sponged with cold water containing a tablespoonful (15 ml) of vinegar.

Do not oil the stiff framework; oil will stain the cover. Instead, slip a sheet of paper between the frame and the cover and spray with a rust inhibitor or rub with a soft lead pencil.

UPHOLSTERY. *See also Furniture*

Upholstered chairs and lounges never go out of style. Regular maintenance will preserve the appearance of the upholstery material and make professional cleaning unnecessary for some time.

Fabric upholstery. Weekly cleaning of fabric upholstery consists of vacuuming, using the special attachment that can be inserted into folds and creases and around piped areas.

An application of spray-on fabric shield will protect new and freshly cleaned fabrics against undue soiling.

Plush velvets and velveteen upholstery should be vacuumed regularly. This is more effective than brushing, which merely redistributes the dust. Use drycleaning fluid occasionally to remove grimy deposits, treating small overlapping areas at a time. Test the effect of the solvent on a small part of the upholstery before proceeding. Modern velvets are often a blend of synthetic fibers. Sponging with a textured cloth wrung out of

Keeping Napped Fabrics Clean

To remove lint, dust, and animal hairs from napped materials, use a clean pure bristle clothes brush lightly dipped in drycleaning fluid.

vinegar water — 1 tablespoonful (15 ml) in 2 cups (500 ml) cold water — is often sufficient to freshen the appearance of these napped fabrics. A steam iron held about 1 inch (3 cm) above crushed velvets will raise the nap.

Acrylic velvets have a built-in grime repellent, and cleaning consists of wiping over the fabric with a napped cloth wrung out of warm detergent suds. Go over the surfaces with a second damp cloth to remove traces of the suds.

Blended silk and rayon upholstery often spots if a drop of liquid falls on it. Sponge the spot with a slightly dampened cloth, working from the outside toward the center. Disturb the outline of the spot by scrubbing gently with your fingernail or an old toothbrush. If the spot is still visible, hold a steam iron just above the mark for a few seconds, then gently scrub the outline again.

Leather upholstery such as cowhide and pigskin needs regular polishing to keep from drying out. Matching leather polish or silicone cream will maintain pliability, gloss, and cleanliness.

To clean neglected dark leather furniture, combine ¼ cup (60 ml) raw linseed oil with ¾ cup (180 ml) vinegar in a lidded jar. Shake well. Apply with a soft cloth and keep changing the cloth as grime, perspiration, and soil marks are loosened.

Cleaning Vinyl Upholstery
Treat grease spots, food spills, perspiration stains, and extra grimy spots on any vinyl upholstery as soon as possible.

Saddle soap is also suitable for washing leather goods. This can be used with warm water. Remove traces of soap with a clean damp cloth.

Dried-out leathers require repeated applications of linseed oil, leather dressing, or petroleum jelly to help restore pliancy. When the dressing is quite absorbed, polish with silicone wax.

Mildew on leather furniture can be removed by working petroleum jelly into the grain and leaving it on for several hours. During damp weather, mildew or mold may form on soiled areas, perhaps where food was spilled. Treat immediately, because it can cause deterioration and bleaching of the leather.

Vinyl upholstery. To clean vinyl upholstery, use a small amount of baking soda or vinegar on a rough rag. Wash the vinyl, using this rag and some mild detergent. Washing vinyl in this way can prevent the hardening and cracking often caused by body oils. Regular wiping with a damp soapy cloth will help to remove traces of perspiration and hair products from the backs of vinyl seats. Perspiration tends to discolor and dry out vinyls.

If the vinyl becomes delustered as a result of any stain removal treatment, rub the area with a little glycerin or apply silicone furniture polish. Make sure that all traces of stain remover have been wiped off, first with a soapy cloth and then with a clean, damp cloth.

VEILS

Wash veils in cool suds. Rinse three times. Dry flat on an old sheet on the lawn; or if ironing is necessary, roll in a towel and iron while slightly damp. Liquid starch will restore crispness.

VELOUR

Usually it is advisable to have velour furnishings and articles drycleaned.

However, if velour is labeled "washable," then wash in as much water as possible. The water should be just warm. Use wool-washing detergent. Shake the articles to remove surface dust. Wash one at a time, squeezing and lifting it in the water to release loosened grime. Rinse twice. Try to choose a fine windy day when drying will be speedy. If possible, hang curtains so that the lines will not leave a mark.

Smooth with a clean clothes brush while drying and shake well when dry to raise the nap. Ironing should not be necessary.

VELVET, VELVETEEN, AND CORDUROY

Silk velvet should be drycleaned. Cotton and synthetic fibers such as rayon and nylon are often washable. The manufacturer's tag on piece goods or the label inside a garment will indicate if drycleaning or washing is desirable.

When washing any napped goods, try to choose a breezy day. Use cool suds and liquid detergent. Move the article around in its bath until it is clean. Do not squeeze or twist; both cause creasing and crushing. Rinse three times, then drip dry. Smooth the pile with a clean clothes brush and shake the garment when it is dry.

Creases can be removed from velvet with steam. Hold a steam iron just above the creases on the wrong side of the material, or hold the underside over a pan of boiling water. You can also hang a velvet garment in a steaming bathroom.

Maroon, brown, bottle-green, navy blue, and red are colors that run. Dye loss is the result of particles suspended in and on the velvet pile.

Dark dyes can be set by pre-soaking the garment in cold water containing 1 rounded tablespoon (15 ml) Epsom salts per 2 quarts (liters) water. Soak for 20 minutes before stripping out the water and washing.

Wash velveteen and corduroy separately in cool detergent suds for the first two or three launderings to avoid tinging other garments. Rinse well and drip-dry, smoothing the pile with a clean clothes brush or your hand while it is still wet.

Ironing is often not necessary. If it is, steam press lightly or hold a steam iron just above the velveteen to raise the pile.

WALLS

There are endless ways to clean your walls, depending on the surface. Walls can be vacuumed, or if very dirty (and washable), you can use an all-purpose cleaner. Remember to wash walls from the bottom to the top. Grimy water drips running from the top of the wall to the bottom, and fortified with a grime-loosening cleaner, will cause traces that are difficult to remove.

To remove tape from a wall, place a cloth over the area and use a warm iron. This will loosen the backing and make it easy to pull off.

Remove finger smudges before they settle in.

Clean brick walls with soap and water; or if they are really dirty, you can try bleach and water. Some stains by the fireplace can be scrubbed with an abrasive cleanser, but you will need to rinse very well to remove all the cleanser.

Wallpaper. Periodic dusting will help to keep all wallpapers more attractive. Use the brush attachment on your vacuum cleaner. If necessary, wash and dry the attachment thoroughly before using on wallpaper to ensure its cleanliness; or, use a freshly washed and dried nylon broom, a soft-bristled wall brush, or a mop covered with an old towel.

Vinyl, spongeable, and washable wallpapers should be dusted before further treatment. Then wring out an absorbent cloth in warm detergent suds and start at the baseboard, working upward in long straight strokes.

Treat one section at a time, completely finishing off that area by going over it a second time with a clean, damp cloth to remove traces of loosened grime and suds. Never overwet wallpaper; even the most washable wallpaper might bubble or lift if it is saturated.

If in doubt about the washability of your wallpaper, test it first in an inconspicuous part of the room. Dust first, then sponge it as described above, rinse, and let it dry. Judge the result carefully: Has the color run? Faded? Has the paper bubbled or lifted?

Stain Removal Tips for Wallpaper

☛ Mix ¼ cup (60 ml) baking soda, ½ cup (125 ml) white vinegar, and 1 cup (250 ml) ammonia. Wash the walls with this solution. Wear rubber gloves.

☛ Use rubbing alcohol, which can sometimes remove black spots from the wall. Test first in an area where it will not show in case discoloration results.

☛ Try a little lighter fluid on a cloth to remove crayon marks. Rub gently.

☛ Some spots can be removed with art gum erasers.

Note: Some wallpaper cannot be washed — check the manufacturer's instructions for care.

Nonwashable papers should be dusted only. Many grime marks can be removed by rubbing them with the inside crust of white bread. Grime and crumbs fall away together, so protect the floor covering by laying down newspapers. On small areas, art gum erasers can be used in the same way.

Detergent makes water wetter. Once the paper is saturated it will be possible to peel it off in large strips.

Removing Wallpaper

To remove old wallpaper easily, go over the surface two or three times with a paint roller saturated in 4 quarts (liters) of hot water containing half a cup (125 ml) of liquid detergent.

Greasy marks can be removed with the aid of absorption and heat. Cover the stain with a white paper towel and press it with a fairly hot iron. As the grease is absorbed into the paper, discard that sheet and use another to avoid redistributing it. Textured papers might require a different treatment. Make a paste of powdered starch, talcum powder, or crushed chalk using a little drycleaning fluid or carbon tetrachloride to mix it. Dab it over the stain and let it dry.

Remove the dry powder by suction with the vacuum cleaner or with a clean clothes brush. Repeat if necessary. If the wallpaper is very dark, test this treatment first on an inconspicuous part of the paper; on some surfaces, traces of the white powder might remain. If necessary, patch the stained area.

Another method to remove grease from wallpaper is to work some rye bread into a ball and put a few drops of kerosene on it. Rub the grease stain gently. To remove crayon from wallpaper, rub with a damp cloth and some toothpaste. Rinse with a clean, damp cloth.

Perspiration and grime on fingers fumbling in the dark for a light switch often leave stains on wallpaper. Rub them with a wad of fresh bread sprinkled with not more than three drops of drycleaning fluid, or protect this vulnerable area with a square of self-adhesive clear plastic.

Pollen from floral arrangements often stains wallpaper. Try to avoid this by keeping fresh flowers away from the paper. The stains can be wiped off vinyl-coated and sealed papers but are usually indelible on those that have not been treated.

Lead pencil can usually be removed with an art gum eraser. Felt pen and ink are sometimes indelible. Some inks and dyes are so fast that a solvent would certainly harm the paper. Patch the area for best results.

Patching Wallpaper
Torn edges are best for patches because cut edges are more clearly defined and they tend to collect dust and darken.

Repapering. When repapering a room, try to save roll ends as well as an entire roll for emergency repairs. It is seldom possible to match old wallpapers because dye lots vary and patterns and colors are constantly replaced.

Wallpaper darkens with exposure, and off-cuts from the roll ends look new and bright by comparison. A more "aged" effect can soon be given to new patches by exposing them to sunlight. Some papers darken quickly; others require a few days to match that on the walls.

Patching wallpaper. Patches are almost invisible if they are applied properly. It is not necessary to remove the stained area, although greasy marks should be sponged with grease solvent before being covered.

Obtain a strip of new paper that is larger in width and breadth than the area to be patched. Cut it roughly into shape, being careful to match the pattern.

Lay the patch face down on a clean surface and tear all around it, making it an uneven shape with tissue-thin edges. Then apply clear paste to the back of the patch, being careful to cover the fine edges. Press it in place, matching the pattern exactly. If necessary, press out air bubbles by rolling over the patch with a rolling-pin or by pressing it with the bristles of a clean clothes brush. A patch applied in this way seldom fails to blend well with the old wallpaper.

WOOL

Woolen garments and articles must be washed carefully. Never use hot water, and do not allow the force of water to strike the garment directly. Use cold or lukewarm water only with soap flakes, mild liquid detergent, or wool-washing detergent. Do not soak woolens. Do not wring, twist, scrub, or rub woolen articles; such action mats the wool fibers and causes felting. Felting removes the elasticity from woven wool, resulting in shrinkage.

Do not dry white woolen garments — particularly fine knits such as babywear — in strong sunlight. This could cause yellowing.

Do not leave wet woolen garments in a heap. Extract surplus water as soon as possible and hang to dry, or spread flat to dry or dry at the lowest temperature in a dryer.

Some woolen garments can be machine washed; some require hand washing. If a short cycle is available on your machine, line the machine with a soft towel that will act as a buffer and will help to keep the woolen garments soft and fluffy. Use cold or lukewarm water and a wool-washing detergent. Remove the garments from the machine as soon as the cycle ends.

Stretch woolens into shape and size while wet, then hang to dry. Sweaters can be hung on old pantyhose, with the legs in the sleeves and the waist and toes pegged to the line. Special plastic-covered hangers are available at department stores.

Before You Buy

Read the care tag on any heavyweight sweater you are planning to buy. Some will specify drycleaning only; others will give specific washing instructions.

Hand-washed woolens can be well rinsed; then, if the timing is right, they can be dropped into a load of clean clothes in a machine approaching the final spin-dry cycle. This will extract surplus water and ensure quicker drying.

Alternatively, roll the garment in a thick towel to absorb extra moisture.

Most synthetic knits will emerge from the wash as new. Others, washed carelessly, will stretch to unwearable proportions.

Shrunken woolens can sometimes be stretched. Dissolve 3 ounces (75 g) Epsom salts in sufficient boiling water to cover the garment. Use a large plastic container or porcelain tub. Do not use a metal container. Allow the solution to cool to body temperature. Soak the dry shrunken garment for half an hour. During that time, keep it submerged and move it around several times. Remove the garment from the solution and roll it in a towel to extract surplus water.

Now unroll the garment and spread it flat. Stretch it methodically lengthwise and crosswise, using a well-fitting garment as a size guide. Hang to dry, using old pantyhose or a plastic-coated hanger. Stretch it several times while it is drying.

When it is almost dry, press it on a well-padded surface with a steam iron on the wool setting, and recheck the measurements.

Do not expect miracles. Some wools respond better than others, but the treatment is inexpensive and worth trying if it might salvage an otherwise valuable wool garment.

Stretched woolens. Some heavy woolens, particularly hand-knits, stretch after they have been laundered. Usually this is because they have been hung on the line while still heavy with water. Crimped wool or loosely knitted wools drop with the weight of the water

Expensive cashmeres and heavy hand-knits will also stretch if you are not careful when washing them.

Shrinking woolens. Sometimes a woolen (but not an acrylic) garment can be shrunk. Lower the dry article into hot, not boiling, water. Let it soak for five minutes, moving it around and keeping all parts under the water. Try to do this in a tub with a plug that can be pulled out to drain the water. Do not lift the garment except in both hands, fully supporting its weight. Press out as much water as possible; then lift it onto a fluffy towel, roll it up in the folds, and press out again. Dry flat, as suggested above, on a sheet on the lawn, or on a warm path. When dry, press lightly with a steam iron using an up-and-down action, not a side-to-side movement.

WORK CLOTHES

Heavily soiled work clothes should not be washed immediately. Dampen them evenly, then rub laundry soap deeply into the stains. Roll the garments tightly, slip them into a large plastic bag, and leave them for about 12 hours.

Wash them the next day in hot detergent suds in the longest cycle of the machine. If the machine is fitted with a pre-wash cycle, use this first, then reset the machine. Hot rinsing will also help to remove stains.

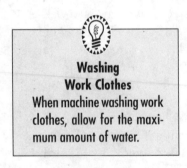

Washing Work Clothes

When machine washing work clothes, allow for the maximum amount of water.

Greasy overalls can be dusted heavily with cheap talcum powder. Scrub it into heavy grease stains with a toothbrush or nailbrush. Roll up the overalls and leave them in a plastic bag for several hours. Shake them outside to remove the powder, which will have absorbed much of the grease, then rub them with soap and treat them as outlined above.

WROUGHT IRON

This is used extensively for garden and patio furniture and for security doors and windows. To clean it, wipe with a cloth dampened with detergent suds. A light spraying with silicone wax will keep the surfaces more dust- and soil-resistant and will help to prevent rust. When repainting becomes necessary, use paint containing a rust inhibitor.

ZINC

Wash with a solution of washing soda and hot water, 1 tablespoon (15 ml) per quart (liter). Rinse and rub with silicone wax.

Part Four

TREATING SPECIFIC STAINS

ACID

Acids can damage fabrics permanently unless treated promptly. Rinse immediately with cold water, holding the stained area under running water so that the acid is flushed out. Spread the stained area over a folded towel and dampen it with household ammonia. Repeat several times, changing the position of the pad. Rinse again under running water. *Note:* Do not use undiluted ammonia on pure wool or silk or on blends containing wool or silk.

Acids on wool or silk should be flushed out with cold water, then sponged with equal parts of ammonia and cold water. Ammonia can restore color to fabrics bleached by acid.

Acid spills on carpets should be blotted up immediately. Fold a number of tissues and put weight on them so that still more acid is absorbed. To neutralize the acid, make a thin paste of baking soda and warm water, then work it deeply into the pile with an old toothbrush. Substitute borax if baking soda is not available. Allow the paste to dry, then sponge with a clean, damp cloth. Repeat the paste application and let it dry again. Vacuum to remove traces of the powder. Repeat the treatment as necessary.

ADHESIVE TAPE

Sponge with eucalyptus, kerosene, or carbon tetrachloride. Finally, wash in warm detergent suds and rinse well.

ALCOHOL, WINE, AND FRUIT BEVERAGES

Alcoholic beverages that have been spilled should be blotted up quickly, and if possible, the stain should be treated before it dries. Sponge immediately with a cloth barely dampened with warm water and containing 1 or 2 drops of liquid detergent. Rinse with a clean, damp cloth and dry as quickly as possible, using a hair dryer set on medium heat.

Spilled alcohol and fruit beverages might be invisible when dry, but stains oxidize with heat and age, and these can become indelible. Sponge or dab with soda water, or sponge with warm water containing a little detergent. Rinse well. Pre-soak dry stains in an enzyme solution and wash in the usual way.

On nonwashable garments, sponge with cold water, then take the stained garment to a drycleaner as soon as possible.

Fabric with dried-on beer stains should be sponged with a solution of equal parts vinegar and dishwashing liquid, then rinsed with warm water.

On carpets, blot up as much as possible immediately. Sponge the area with a clean towel wrung out of warm water. Then dissolve 1 teaspoon (5 ml) of laundry detergent powder in 1 cup (250 ml) warm water and use the solution to lightly wet a piece of toweling. Repeatedly sponge the stained area, blotting up with dry cloths as you work. Sponge with a series of damp cloths to remove the suds. Blot as dry as possible, then train a low-set hair dryer or an electric fan over the damp spot. Smooth the pile. New spills are sometimes barely visible, but as the stain ages it becomes brown and then it will be very difficult to remove.

To remove alcohol from carpets, blot up the spill as quickly as possible, continuing until the cloth or tissues remain dry. Mix 1 tablespoon (15 ml) of laundry detergent in 2 cups (500 ml) warm water. Sponge this into the stain, using dry tissues or cloths to blot up as you work so that the carpet does not become too wet. Sponge and blot repeatedly. Be thorough; these stains become brown and indelible with age unless they are completely removed.

On a light-colored carpet, a weak bleach solution can be used to sponge out remaining traces of the spill. Use 1 teaspoon (5 ml) bleach to ¼ cup (60 ml) cold water. Finally, sponge with clean, damp cloths and train an electric fan on the area to dry it quickly.

For red wine, blot immediately with tissues. Then make a thick paste of borax and cold water, and work it deeply into the pile with a toothbrush or nailbrush. Let the paste dry, then vacuum. Repeat as often as necessary.

Alcohol-based drinks, perfumes, and medicines attack the wood finish on furniture. Blot up the spill as quickly as possible, trying not to worsen the stain. Sponge the stain with a clean, damp cloth and blot dry; then assess the damage. If the furniture has been well maintained, the mark will be slight. Rub hard with silicone polish, working from the outside of the mark toward the center. Rub well, following the grain, with linseed oil or petroleum jelly mixed with cigarette ash. After rubbing hard for several minutes, smear the area with oil or petroleum jelly and leave this on for at least 12 hours. Then wipe it off and polish in the usual way.

ANIMAL HAIRS

Some upholstery fabrics seem to act as magnets for animal hairs. Concentrated vacuuming is best, of course, but periodic cleaning is easier with a slightly dampened sponge or a clean, damp chamois cloth. Clothes brushes are also effective — they consist of a velvet pad with a handle and induce static electricity when they are used.

ANTIPERSPIRANTS AND DEODORANTS

Antiperspirants that contain aluminum chloride are acidic and may interact with some fabric dyes. Color can be restored by sponging with ammonia. Rinse thoroughly. To use on wool, mohair, or silk, dilute ammonia with an equal amount of water.

Another method for removing deodorant stains is to apply rubbing alcohol to the stain and cover the area with an absorbent pad dampened with alcohol. Keep both moist and let sit.

Treat stiffened, yellowed areas with an enzyme-soaking powder. Make a stiff paste of the powder by mixing it with cold water. Rub it into the stained sections. Colored articles should be pre-tested in an inconspicuous part of the garment to see if the color is affected by the paste.

Slip the garment into a plastic bag and leave it for 8 or more hours.

These treated areas must then be washed in very hot water. Hot water might cause wrinkling or creasing in a drip-dry garment, so stretch only the stained sections over a basin in the sink and pour over each underarm about 1 quart (liter) of very hot water. Then wash the whole garment by hand or in a machine in the usual way.

Do not iron material with a deodorant stain. The heat will interact with the chemical residue from the deodorant and the fabric could be ruined.

BABY FORMULA STAINS

Some milk and baby formula stains can be removed using unflavored meat tenderizer. Make a paste of the tenderizer and cool water, rub it into the stain, and let sit before washing as usual. This treatment is effective because meat tenderizers contain an enzyme that breaks down protein.

BERRIES *(blueberries, cranberries, raspberries, strawberries)*

Dried berry stains on washables should be rubbed on each side with bar soap. Then cover with a thick mixture of cornstarch and cold water. Rub in well, then leave fabric in the sun until the stain disappears. Repeat the process in three days if needed.

Another way to treat berry stains is to sponge the area with lemon juice (or rub a lemon slice over the stain). Flush with water and allow to air dry. For persistent stains, soak item in a solution of 1 teaspoon (5 ml) mild detergent, 1 teaspoon (5 ml) white vinegar, and 1 quart (liter) warm water for at least 15 minutes. Launder as usual. (See also Fruit.)

BEVERAGES

Blot up immediately until the mark is as dry as possible. Then sponge with clean, warm water containing borax — 1 teaspoon (5 ml) per cup (250 ml) of water. Avoid overwetting. Sponge and blot repeatedly. See entries for specific beverages.

BLOOD

On washable fabrics, soak as soon as possible in salted water, or soak in an enzyme pre-soaking solution, if necessary, for 2 or 3 hours. Wash in cool suds or in cold water in a machine. Traces of the stain can be bleached in either liquid or powdered bleach depending on the fabric involved. Read labeled instructions carefully. You can also sponge with hydrogen peroxide (1 part of hydrogen peroxide to 3 parts of water) and expose the stain to fresh air, keeping moist with peroxide until the stain fades. Rinse well to remove traces of peroxide. Have good garments drycleaned.

Sponge mattresses with hydrogen peroxide and keep damp with peroxide until the stain fades.

Fresh bloodstains can sometimes be removed from washable fabrics with a solution of ½ teaspoon (2 ml) salt and 1 cup (250 ml) water. Soak the item in cold water with laundry detergent. Fresh bloodstains on white cotton fabrics should be soaked in cold water with ammonia.

If you have blood on the carpet, blot with tissues. Sponge with salted water — 1 teaspoon (5 ml) to 1 cup (250 ml) cold water. Sponge and blot until the mark fades. Sponge with a clean, damp cloth to remove traces of salt. If a stain remains, mix equal parts of peroxide and warm water, and work this into the pile with a toothbrush. Keep slightly damp for 1 or 2 hours until the stain fades, then sponge again with a clean, damp cloth. Another way to treat bloodstains on the carpet is to make a paste of borax and water or powdered bleach and water and let it dry on the pile. Vacuum to remove the dried powder.

If the blood has dried, dampen it with a little water. Sponge with laundry detergent solution — 1 teaspoon (5 ml) powdered detergent to 1 cup (250 ml) tepid water. Sponge and blot repeatedly until the mark fades. If the carpet is light, apply the peroxide treatment described above. ***Note:*** Avoid excessive wetting.

BURN MARKS. *See also Scorch Marks*

Remove attachment from the end of the vacuum cleaner pipe and concentrate the suction over the burn. This will remove much of the charred pile. Mix 1 teaspoon (5 ml) laundry detergent powder in ½ cup (125 ml) water, and gently scrub the burn with an old toothbrush, using this solution. Blot up excess dampness and sponge again with a damp cloth. To remove remaining burn marks, lightly bleach with equal parts of peroxide and water, plus one single drop of ammonia. When this dries, sponge again with a damp cloth; if necessary, carefully snip charred pile ends with nail scissors.

Burn marks on the polished surfaces of furniture might need the expertise of a professional polisher. However, you can cover with petroleum jelly or a drop of oil until metal polish can be rubbed in with a circular movement. Wipe this off and cover again with linseed, camphorated, or olive oil or more petroleum jelly. Leave this on for 24 hours. Rub again, wipe off, and polish.

Burn marks on fabric upholstery can be camouflaged by inserting a piece of material cut from under the furniture, carefully matched, and eased under the hole with a knitting needle. Use a little fabric adhesive around the edges of the patch to keep it in position. First remove charred edges around the hole with fine nail scissors. When the patch is in position, cover the spot with waxed paper, apply a weight, and leave it there until the adhesive dries.

Small burn holes and cuts on vinyl upholstery can be treated by cutting a larger patch of matching vinyl from a fold underneath the chair or lounge. Trim the edges of the burn with a razor blade or nail scissors to remove the char mark. Smear a polyvinyl chloride (PVC) adhesive around the margins of the patch, and slip it under the hole with a knitting needle. Wipe off any excess adhesive with acetone, nail polish remover, or carbon tetrachloride before it sets; then cover the patch with a sheet of waxed paper and apply a weight for several hours.

BUTTER AND MARGARINE

Gently scrape up any solid matter with a blunt knife.

For washable articles, dampen the stain. Rub powder detergent into the marks and scrub between two thumbs. Wash and dry. If the stain remains, spread it over a folded pad and sponge it with a cloth dampened with drycleaning fluid. Air to dry. Repeat if necessary, then wash and rinse.

Fabrics with special finishes such as drip-dry and wash-and-wear tend to retain grease stains, so patience and repeated applications of fluid over a series of clean pads might be required. Do not iron until all traces of the stain have been removed. Age and heat will cause yellowing, and the marks will be indelible.

Nonwashable articles should be taken to a drycleaner.

After scraping as much of the solid butter as you can, apply an absorbent powder. Do not press the absorbent into the fabric. Let it sit until it cakes, then lightly brush the loose material off. Repeat if necessary.

For butter on carpets, remove as much as possible with a pliable spatula or knife. Sponge lightly with drycleaning fluid, blotting with tissues as the grease dissolves. Then treat the area with carpet shampoo or sprinkle dry carpet-cleaning powder over the stain; leave it on for several hours, then vacuum.

CANDLE WAX

Lift off solid wax. Place folded tissues under and over the remaining mark and a sheet of brown paper over the top tissue, and press with a warm iron. Repeat until no more melted wax is absorbed by the tissues. Or hold fabric taut over the sink, and pour boiling water through the fabric from a height to flush away wax. Take care not to burn yourself.

Sponge the remaining grease mark with drycleaning fluid or a similar solvent, working over a folded towel. Wash in the usual way.

Candle wax stains on linens should be rubbed with vegetable oil. Wipe off excess oil with a clean cloth, then wash as usual. To remove a lot of candle wax, scrape excess wax off the fabric. Put fabric between layers of paper towels or paper bags, and press with a warm iron.

Note: Minimal heat should transfer the wax to the towel or paper. Afterward, use a cleaning solution on the remaining stain.

To remove candle wax from carpets, press an ice cube on the wax drip to harden the wax so it can be pulled up. Treat stain with drycleaning fluid. Let dry and vacuum.

Lift off as much as possible. Cover the remaining wax with half a dozen tissues and press with a cool iron. Change the tissue and repeat until no more wax is absorbed. The dye from colored candles might leave a stain; sponge this with carbon tetrachloride unless the pile is set in rubber or synthetic rubber. If it is, make a paste of powdered starch, talcum powder, or cornstarch and drycleaning fluid. Work this into the pile, vacuuming the area when the powder dries.

Wax on a polished surface can be removed without scratching the furniture if the wax is first made brittle and hard. To do this, put a tray of ice cubes in a plastic bag and let this stand on the wax for 2 or 3 minutes. Then cover the blade of a blunt knife with a piece of soft cloth and gently lift and scrape off the wax. Rub the marks with a damp cloth and a smear of soap. Sponge with a clean cloth and polish in the usual way.

CANDY

To remove candy stains from carpets, scrape up as much material as you can. Mix 1 teaspoon (5 ml) mild detergent, 1 teaspoon (5 ml) white vinegar, and 1 quart (liter) warm water. Apply to stain, let dry, then vacuum. For removing chocolate stains, see Chocolate.

CARBON PAPER

Sponge with carbon tetrachloride, working over a folded towel that will absorb loosened dye. Let this dampness evaporate, then dampen the mark and rub in a little detergent. Scrub lightly between two thumbs; rinse under a running cold water tap. Wash in the usual way.

Nonwashables should be taken to a cleaner. To treat them at home, try sponging them with carbon tetrachloride over an absorbent pad. Work first from the back of the stain so that it is flushed out into the pad, the position of which should be changed frequently to avoid restaining the garment.

CHOCOLATE OR COCOA

Remove excess chocolate from the stained area without embedding the chocolate deeper into the material. Sponge with cold water or soak for 30 minutes in an enzyme pre-wash solution. Rub detergent into the remaining stain and scrub it lightly between your two thumbs. Rinse out loosened traces under cold running water and dry. If a greasy mark remains, sponge it with a solvent such as drycleaning fluid. The final stain should come out in the wash.

For nonwashables, flush the stain with club soda to prevent setting. Sponge the area with a drycleaning solvent. If stain persists, apply a few drops of dishwashing detergent and a few drops of ammonia to the stain, then scrape. Blot occasionally with an absorbent pad. Flush well with water to remove ammonia.

To remove chocolate from carpets, blot up as much as possible, then sponge with 1 teaspoon (5 ml) powdered laundry detergent dissolved in 1 cup (250 ml) warm water. Scrub the suds into the pile with a toothbrush if the stain is deep. Sponge and blot with dry tissues or cloths until the stain fades. Final traces will disappear if a paste of borax and warm water is worked into the pile and left to dry. Vacuum the area and repeat as necessary. If the beverage contains milk, sponging with drycleaning fluid might be necessary. Follow this treatment with more sponging, first with detergent suds, then with a clean, damp cloth to remove the suds.

Note: Drycleaning fluid should not come in contact with rubber or synthetic backing. Instead, make a paste of powdered starch and the drycleaner, and work this into the pile.

COFFEE AND TEA

Blot up quickly and rinse out or sponge out as much as possible with cool water. Rub detergent into the stain and scrub between your two thumbs before washing in the usual way.

If a stain remains and if the fabric will stand boiling water, spread the stain over a basin in the sink, cover it with borax, and pour on boiling water. Let the stain soak in the borax water for 30 minutes.

If the fabric will not stand boiling water, make a thick paste of borax and hot water and rub it into the stain. Leave it on for half an hour, then brush off the paste. Repeat as often as necessary.

Diluted peroxide can be used on white or light fabrics to remove final traces of the stain. Keep the mark dampened with equal parts of water and peroxide in sunlight for 2 hours or longer. Rinse to remove traces of peroxide.

To remove coffee or tea stains from china, wet the cup with white vinegar. Dip a damp rag in baking soda or salt and wipe the stain out.

Denture-cleaning tablets will remove coffee or tea stains from a cup. Drop a tablet in the cup of warm water, and let it soak for several hours. Gentle scrubbing will remove the stains. Wash and rinse cups thoroughly after treatment.

To remove coffee stains from carpet, blot the spill as soon as possible. Mix 1 teaspoon (5 ml) mild detergent, 1 teaspoon (5 ml) white vinegar, and 1 quart (liter) warm water. Apply to stain, then let dry. Follow with an application of drycleaning fluid. Allow carpet to dry, then vacuum.

COLA AND SOFT DRINKS

A soft drink spilled on a carpet might be invisible initially, but it must be treated promptly and thoroughly, because when stains age they may become indelible.

Blot the area until no more of the stain can be absorbed. Then sponge deeply into the pile with laundry detergent powder (not liquid detergent), using a toothbrush or nailbrush if necessary. Avoid excessive wetting; blot with tissues or clean cloths as you work. Finally, sponge out the suds with a series of clean, damp cloths and when the area is dry, vacuum thoroughly.

COSMETICS

Dampen the stain and rub in powdered detergent, or rub undiluted liquid detergent into the dry stain. Scrub between both thumbs, then rinse under cold running water. Repeat several times if necessary before washing as usual.

Send nonwashable garments to a drycleaner.

CRAYON

To remove crayon stains from fabrics, scrape off excess material. Sponge detergent onto the stain, rinse, then dry. Persistent stains can be sponged with a cleaning fluid.

Crayon stains on acrylic, cotton, linen, polyester, nylon, and washable wool can be removed by placing the stained area between two pieces of white blotting paper and pressing with a warm iron. The blotting paper should be changed as the stain is absorbed. Take care not to spread the stain. If a stain from the crayon color remains, flush the area with drycleaning solvent.

Another method for removing crayon stains is to place the stained surface down on several paper towels. Spray with a petroleum-based solvent and let stand for several minutes. Turn the fabric and spray the other side; let stand. Apply detergent and work into stained area until the stain is gone. Hand wash the item in detergent to remove traces of the oil. Wash as usual.

Use silicone spray to remove crayon from countertops.

DYE

Dye stains are difficult to remove, especially if the entire garment cannot be soaked in a suitable bleach.

Try spreading the stain over a large basin in an unplugged sink or tub. Turn on the cold water faucet so that a steady drip (not flow) falls on the stain. Empty the basin as it fills. Often a dye stain will vanish after 3 or 4 hours of this treatment.

Some dye stains respond to a long soak in rich, cool suds.

Articles that can be bleached should be soaked in a weak bleach solution in a nonmetal container for 6 to 8 hours. Care should be taken not to expose treated fabrics (drip-dry, wash-and-wear, noniron, and so on) to chlorine bleach.

Other stains may respond to sponging with equal parts of water and peroxide. Expose the dye stain to air or sunlight and keep it moist with peroxide solution until the stain disappears. Rinse well.

Clothing stained with hair dye should be washed in sudsy water with vinegar added. White items can later be bleached.

If the color from an item in the washing machine has run onto other items, and the items discolored were originally white or light colored, try a commercial dye remover.

EGG

Scrape off any solid matter. Soak in a nonmetal container with an enzyme-soaking compound for as long as convenient — 6 to 8 hours if possible. If a stain remains, rub in powdered detergent and rub between both thumbs. Rinse and wash in the usual way. The stain must be totally removed before heat is applied.

Nonwashable garments should be drycleaned without delay. Be sure to advise the cleaner as to the origin of the stain.

If treating at home, dampen the stain and rub in undiluted liquid detergent. Rub between both thumbs. Spread over a pad, and sponge repeatedly with a series of damp cloths to remove the suds.

To remove egg from carpet, scrape up as much as possible and sponge the stain with salty water using ½ teaspoon (2 ml) to 1 cup (250 ml) cool water. Then sponge with a solution of enzyme laundry stain remover, followed by sponging with a series of clean, damp cloths. Blot frequently with dry cloths or tissues to absorb excess moisture.

FOOD DYE

Fruit juices, gelatin desserts, and frozen fruit treats are just a few of the foods that leave stubborn food dye stains. If you are able to treat the stain while it is still fresh, neutralize it with a solution of 1 tablespoon (15 ml) ammonia in a cup of water. This will especially help prevent dye transfer on nylon carpeting and similar fabrics. Then rub table salt into the stain and let it sit. Remove salt, repeat if necessary, then rinse.

Stretch a small stain under cold running water and turn it on full. The force of the water will flush out much of the dye without spreading the stain. Then rub in powdered detergent and scrub between both thumbs. Rinse again under cold running water. Soak in cool detergent suds for 30 minutes, and wash in the usual way. If a stain remains and if the basic color of the garment will not be bleached by peroxide (pretest on an inside seam), keep the stain moist with equal parts of water and hydrogen peroxide in sunlight until it fades. Rinse well.

FRUIT. *See also Berries*

These stains must be removed *before* the article is washed. Heat and age will set fruit stains and make them indelible. Sponge or spray with soda water immediately.

Rinse the stain as soon as possible while it is still wet. Rub in detergent and scrub the stain between both thumbs. Rinse under running water as hot as the fabric can stand. Hold the material taut so that the full flow of water pours onto the stain.

If the stain is still visible, make a paste of borax and warm water and work it into the stained fibers. Let this dry, then brush it off. Repeat several times if necessary.

On all washable, colored garments, sponge the fresh stain with cold water. Half-fill a basin with boiling water and add 1 tablespoon (15 ml) ammonia. Stretch the stained section taut across the top of the basin. Let the fumes permeate the stain; do not let the material touch the water. Test the effect of peroxide on an unseen part of the garment. If the dye is unaffected, pour a few drops of diluted peroxide onto the stain with the steam still rising. Lift off and keep moist with peroxide until the stain fades. *Note:* If ammonia, peroxide, and glycerin must be purchased, it will be more economical to take the garment to a drycleaner. Be sure to advise the cleaner of the cause of the stain.

Fresh fruit stains, treated promptly, usually come out in the wash. It is important to sponge them while they are fresh, especially peach, citrus, and the sap from banana palms.

Old fruit stains. Reconstitute the stain with glycerin. Leave this on for half an hour, then treat as above.

Glycerin rubbed into a dried stain will freshen it and make it easier to remove. Then treat as above, according to the material. Nonwashables are best treated as soon as possible by a drycleaner. Sponge the stains with cold water as soon as they occur, and take the garment promptly to a cleaner. Be sure to explain the nature of the stain.

To remove from carpets, scrape up as much of the spilled material as you can. Mix 1 teaspoon (5 ml) mild detergent, 1 teaspoon (5 ml) white vinegar, and 1 quart (liter) warm water. Apply to stain, let dry, then vacuum. Repeat if necessary.

FRUIT JUICES AND CORDIALS

To remove from carpets, blot up as much as possible, then sponge with fresh effervescent soda water, blotting frequently. If a stain remains, sponge with 1 teaspoon (5 ml) powdered detergent dissolved in 1 cup (250 ml) water, scrubbing it in with a toothbrush or nailbrush dipped in the solution. Avoid excess wetting and blot frequently. Sponge with clean, damp cloths. These stains will become brown and often indelible with age, so all traces should be removed quickly.

Old stains need to be reconstituted with glycerin. Rub in a little glycerin and leave it on for half an hour, then sponge with the detergent solution as suggested above. A warm water and borax paste worked into the stained area will often remove final traces of the spill.

FURNITURE POLISH

To remove from carpets, blot up immediately and continue to blot until no more is absorbed by cloths or tissues. Sponge with powdered detergent, 1 teaspoon (5 ml) dissolved in 1 cup (250 ml) tepid water. Work it into the carpet pile with a toothbrush or nailbrush, and blot up with fresh tissues as you work. Then sponge with a clean, damp cloth to remove traces of the suds.

Furniture polish usually contains dye, and this can be difficult to remove. If the stained area is large and conspicuous, call for professional help.

Smaller, lighter stains will respond to a light application of drycleaning fluid. Blot up as you sponge to remove traces of dye and oil. Avoid overuse of the fluid as it could damage the back of rubber or synthetic rubber pile or remove loose dyes. If in doubt, pre-test on an inconspicuous part of the carpet.

GLUE, MUCILAGE, AND ADHESIVES

Modern adhesives are difficult to remove. If you need to purchase solvents, you might find that it is more economical to have the garments drycleaned. Tell the cleaner the name of the adhesive that caused the stain.

Balsa wood (model airplane) glue. This can be removed from most fabrics with acetone.

To remove this glue from furniture, try rubbing with cold cream or vegetable oil.

Plastic adhesives. Try to treat the stain before it dries. Wash in cool detergent suds. If a stain remains, bring ¼ cup (60 ml) of white vinegar to boiling point and immerse the stain. Have another ¼ cup (60 ml) of white vinegar on the stove and as the first cools, reheat it while the stain soaks in the hot vinegar. Continue this process for 15 minutes.

Rubber cements. Gently scrape up solid matter. Spread stain over a pad and sponge with carbon tetrachloride or drycleaning fluid. *Note:* All these substances are flammable, so observe fire precautions.

Rubber cement on furniture can sometimes be removed by rubbing with cold cream or vegetable oil.

Other glues. Sponge or rinse in warm water. Rub in powdered detergent and scrub the area between two thumbs. Rinse and wash in water as hot as the fabric will stand.

Soap and water will remove most synthetic glue if the stain is fresh. Acetone will dissolve most clear plastic cements, but you should pre-test on fabric. *Note:* Acetone cannot be used on acetate.

For an old or dried glue stain, soak the fabric in a boiling solution of vinegar and water — 1 part vinegar to 10 parts water — for 30 minutes. Water-rinseable paint and varnish remover will remove some model cements but should be tested on the fabric first.

If a water-soluble glue caused the stain, sponge with warm water and soap to remove as much as possible. If the stain is old or dried water-soluble glue, soak in water as hot as the fabric will allow. Remove the glue carefully as it softens in the water.

To remove from carpets, scrape up as much as possible with a knife or spatula. Sponge first with a cloth dampened with hot water, then with heated vinegar. Blot frequently to remove traces of dissolved glue.

There are many types of glues and adhesives, some of which might be damaging to synthetic carpets. Acetone may be effective on natural fibers, but always test these agents first on an inconspicuous part of the carpet. If in doubt, don't hesitate to call a professional cleaner.

GRASS AND FLOWERS

Grass stains in washable fabrics can be removed by rubbing laundry detergent into the stained area and rinsing.

If the fabric is not washable, dampen the stained area with rubbing alcohol. Test first for colorfastness. Dilute alcohol with 2 parts water for acetate fabrics. Do not use alcohol on wool. Rinse. If stain persists, sponge with vinegar, then with water. Rinse.

Avoid alkalis such as ammonia, degreasers, or alkaline detergents on grass stains. They interact with the tannin in grass stains and can permanently set the stain.

GRAVY

To remove from carpets, wipe up as much of the spilled material as possible. Mix 1 teaspoon (5 ml) mild detergent, 1 teaspoon (5 ml) white vinegar, and 1 quart (liter) warm water. Apply to stain, let dry, then vacuum. Apply drycleaning fluid, let carpet dry, then vacuum again.

GREASE AND OIL

Grease, whether it is from automotive, vegetable, or animal oil, can leave a semitransparent stain that turns dark from all the soil it picks up. To remove a grease stain, first gently remove as much of the greasy substance as possible without further embedding the substance in the fabric. Apply an absorbent agent. Let the agent sit until it cakes with the greasy material. Gently brush away the absorbent, and repeat if necessary.

Spread the stained area face down over a thickly folded cloth and work from the back of the stain so that dissolved grease is absorbed into the pad rather than deeper into the fabric.

Sponge with drycleaning fluid or carbon tetrachloride. Change the position of the pad as it becomes stained. Let the dampness evaporate; repeat the treatment over a fresh pad.

Grease stains can set, and with age and heat they can develop into a yellow stain. Depending on the fabric, this can be treated with bleach or with peroxide suitably diluted. Treated fabrics (for example, those with noniron or crease-resistant finishes) retain grease marks and require longer treatment than others.

Nonwashables. Dryclean or, if prepared to exercise time and patience, sponge repeatedly with small amounts of drycleaning solvent. Change the absorbent pad frequently to avoid restaining the garment.

Washables. For washable fabrics, scrub with distilled or soft water and soap.

To remove food spills from carpets, scrape and blot up as much as possible. Sponge with powdered detergent, 1 teaspoon (5 ml) dissolved in 1 cup (250 ml) warm water, blotting up as you work; then apply drycleaning fluid, being careful not to wet the carpet backing. Finally, sponge with a damp cloth.

Light, greasy marks can often be treated with dry carpet cleaner worked well into the pile and left for several hours. Use the vacuum cleaner to remove the powder.

Bicycle grease. Cover with tissues and stand on them; the tissues will absorb some of the grease. Sponge with eucalyptus or with a little kerosene, blotting frequently as you work. Work from the outer rim of the stain toward the center. Try not to make the stain larger. Sponge with an old towel dipped in powdered laundry detergent dissolved in warm water, 1 teaspoon (5 ml) to 1 cup (250 ml) water. Blot frequently. If a stain remains, apply 2 or 3 applications of borax powder mixed to a paste with warm water, removing each dry application with the vacuum cleaner before reapplying.

For heavy and dark grease stains, call a professional.

Grease marks on upholstery can be absorbed with powdered chalk (not crayon), powdered starch, or talcum powder.

The white absorbents (starch and talcum powder) cause no problems on light-colored upholsteries, but on darker colors they can be difficult to remove. Crush a matching stick of chalk (from a stationery store) finely with a hammer, and rub this powder in. Another option is to fold it up in an old handkerchief, lay it over a grease stain, then press with a moderately hot iron.

An old grease stain, dried and soiled, can be treated with a paste made from one of the absorbents and a cleaning solvent such as carbon tetrachloride or drycleaning fluid. Spread this over the stain and let it dry. Vacuum or brush it away. Vacuuming is preferable; brushing will scatter the powder.

GUM

Harden soft chewing gum before you try to remove it. One way to do this is to put the fabric in the freezer. Scrape off hard residue, and remove the stain with vinegar, dishwashing liquid, or lighter fluid.

Peanut butter will soften old or dry gum for removal, but it may leave an oily spot that will in turn need to be treated (see Grease and Oil).

For carpets, slip a tray full of ice cubes into a watertight plastic bag and stand this over the gum for a few minutes. The gum will become brittle and pieces will be easy to lift off. Snip off small stubborn pieces with nail scissors. Remove traces of the gum with carbon tetrachloride or drycleaning fluid applied *lightly* to the pile, particularly if the backing is rubber or synthetic rubber.

Remove chewing gum from upholstered surfaces by freezing it. Put a trayful of ice cubes into a watertight plastic bag and rest it on the gum. Soon it will become brittle and much of it can be peeled off. Sponge out remaining stains with carbon tetrachloride or drycleaning fluid.

HAND CREAM

To remove from carpets, wipe up spilled material. Apply drycleaning fluid and let carpet dry. Repeat if necessary. Vacuum.

HARD-WATER STAINS

Hard-water stains result from minerals in the water. Old stains and deposits can be thick and tough to remove. Use a cleaner with at least 9 percent phosphoric acid. Apply and allow to soak for several minutes. Repeat until the stain is gone.

To prevent further hard-water stains, consider a water softener, or apply lemon oil after cleaning to prevent buildup.

HEAT MARKS

Heat marks on furniture are usually caused by placing hot plates, teapots, coffee pots, casserole dishes, and so forth on an unprotected table. Treat in the same way as you would water marks on furniture, repeating the treatment several times as necessary.

ICE CREAM

Sponge with cold water or soda water as soon as possible, or place article in an enzyme-soaking solution for half an hour. Wash in the usual way. If a greasy mark remains, sponge it with grease solvent such as drycleaning fluid or carbon tetrachloride. Work over a padded cloth that will absorb loosened grease elements.

To remove from carpets, scrape up as much as possible with a spatula or knife. Sponge with tepid laundry detergent suds. Avoid excessive wetting and blot with tissues as you work. Sponge with damp cloths. If a greasy mark still persists, sponge with drycleaning fluid, being careful not to wet the backing if it is rubber or synthetic rubber. Or you can make a paste of borax and water and work that into the pile. When the paste dries, vacuum the area.

INK

Sponge ballpoint ink stains with alcohol or a cleaning fluid. Sometimes hair spray will remove ballpoint ink from hands, leather, or plastic. Spray it directly onto the stain, rub it in, and rinse.

Hair spray sometimes removes ballpoint ink stains from clothing, but you should test it on an inconspicuous area of the item first. Hold a cloth under the stain to collect the ink, then spray directly onto the stain.

Use acetone on fabrics (but not on acetate). Some ink can be washed out. Test by staining a scrap of similar material with the same ink. Let it dry and wash in the usual way, or spray it with a pre-wash stain remover when it is dry and wash it as usual.

To remove ballpoint ink from leather, rub petroleum jelly on the spot and leave it for several days before wiping clean.

Some inks can be treated with turpentine. Work over thickly folded cloths or a folded towel. Spread the stain face down and sponge the back of it with turpentine, or use an old toothbrush with a tapping rather than a scrubbing action to drive the dissolved ink into the pad. Change the pad frequently as it becomes stained. Flush under water as hot as the fabric can stand. Rub in powdered detergent and scrub between both thumbs. Rinse and wash.

The manufacturers of some inks recommend specific solvents, so read the label on the ink bottle and follow instructions for removing stains caused by the ink involved. The recommended solvent will be more effective than others.

To remove ballpoint ink from carpets, immediately apply drycleaning fluid and let carpet dry. Repeat until stain comes out. Vacuum when dry. Use care when applying drycleaning solvents to carpets with rubber or synthetic rubber backings.

On a light carpet, make a paste of cream of tartar and lemon juice and work this into the pile. Leave it on for one minute, then sponge and responge. Blot dry.

White vinyl upholstery is a temptation to young children, who will mar these surfaces with ballpoint scribblings. The most effective first aid for this stain is ordinary saliva. Applied immediately and generously to fresh ballpoint marks, many such stains can be wiped off with a clean cloth.

First wipe over the area with glycerin. This helps reconstitute the stain, thus making it easier to remove. Leave the glycerin on for half an hour, then try one or more of the following, wiping off between treatments.

➤ Eucalyptus. Apply it with a white cloth. Persevere if the cloth becomes stained with ink, a sign that it is coming away.

➤ Acetone, usually found in nail polish remover, available in drugstores.

➤ Hydrogen peroxide. Add 1 drop of cloudy ammonia to 1 teaspoon (5 ml) peroxide.

➤ Commercial stain remover.

Pre-test on an unseen part of the upholstery. Mark an inconspicuous section with similar ink, then dampen it with acetone or nail polish remover. Immediately blot up the loosened ballpoint ink with a tissue.

This will show whether the covering would be damaged by the application of acetone; if so, substitute eucalyptus or a commercial stain remover, still experimenting on the test piece.

LACQUER

Fold several cloths or a towel and slip it under the stain to act as an absorbent pad. Sponge the stain with acetone, working from the back of it so that dissolved lacquer is flushed into the pad. *Note:* Do not use acetone on acetates.

If a solvent needs to be purchased, it might prove more economical to take the garment to a drycleaner. Tell the cleaner the name of the lacquer involved.

LINT

Sometimes an item goes through the wash with a tissue left in the pocket, leaving dark clothing covered with lint after it has been through the washing machine. To remove the lint, dampen an old handkerchief with fabric softener and put it with the articles in the dryer. Run the dryer for 5 minutes on a warm setting. Most of the lint will be caught up in the filter, and the remainder can be brushed off with a clothes brush.

Some dark fabrics seem to act as a magnet to lint, and this is particularly the case in a washing machine. Remove tissues from pockets, clean out the lint filter, and wash dark items together. Lint can be removed by hard brushing with a piece of dampened sponge or with a corrugated clothes brush, which generates static electricity when it is drawn sharply over the surface thereby attracting lint particles to its own surface.

However, much lint in the wash can be avoided if these simple rules are followed:

➤ Do not wash dark fabrics with white or light-colored clothing.

➤ Turn pockets inside out, and turn down cuffs and brush them before putting them in a machine. These are repositories for lint and, like a single paper tissue, can speckle an entire load of dark clothing.

➤ Chenille spreads and garments, towels, babies' diapers, and washable mats are typical lint creators. Wash these separately or in one load, certainly not with dark clothing in the same load.

➤ Use plenty of water when hand or machine washing. Do not overload the washer or the tub. Rinse well.

➤ Wash synthetic items (such as nylon and velveteen clothing) inside out so they will attract less lint.

LIPSTICK

Lipstick is dye in an oily base. Water or heat or wet spotters will spread and set the stain. Rub in vegetable oil or mineral oil and let sit for 15 minutes. Sponge in a few drops of ammonia (unless the fabric is silk or wool). If the stain is old and has dried, apply petroleum jelly and wait 30 minutes.

Hair spray can be used to remove lipstick stains from clothing (test on an inconspicuous area of the item first). Spray directly onto stain, let sit for a few minutes, then wipe off gently.

To remove lipstick from carpets, carefully scrape up or lift off solid matter. If it is very soft, slip a trayful of ice cubes into a plastic bag and rest it over the mark for a few minutes. The cold will harden the lipstick and pieces will lift off.

Mix enzyme stain removing and pre-soak powder into a stiff paste with water and spread it over the mark. Leave it on for 5 minutes, then lift it off with a pliable knife. Sponge repeatedly with detergent solution — ½ teaspoon (2 ml) of powdered detergent in ½ cup (125 ml) water — continually blotting with fresh tissues as the stain is loosened. Then sponge with eucalyptus sprinkled onto a piece of old toweling. Continue this process until all the color is removed. Sponge with a clean, damp cloth.

MAYONNAISE

To remove mayonnaise from carpets, scrape up as much as possible. Sponge with effervescing soda water, blotting up quickly. Sponge out remaining stains with powdered detergent solution — 1 teaspoon (5 ml) to 1 cup (250 ml) water — then sponge with clean, damp cloths. If an oil stain persists, sponge lightly with carbon tetrachloride or drycleaning fluid, using caution if the pile is set in a rubber or synthetic backing.

MEAT JUICES

These are difficult to remove once they have dried. Sponge with cold water, or soak in an enzyme pre-soaking solution for half an hour after rubbing some of the pre-soak powder into the dampened stain and scrubbing between two thumbs. Wash in the usual way, but in cool water.

Nonwashables. Sponge with cold water. Take to a cleaner.

MEDICINES

These differ greatly in composition. If the garment is good, take it to a cleaner, along with a piece of material deliberately stained with the same medicine (to use as a tester).

Syrupy medicines can usually be washed out with water. Dampen the stain and rub in detergent, or pre-soak in an enzyme solution before washing.

Spills on bedding or other articles not worth drycleaning should be sponged or soaked at once.

Oily medicines can be treated with a grease solvent.

Medicines that contain iron often cause rusty marks. Treat the stain as a rust mark (see Rust), or check your local hardware store for commercial rust-removing products.

Medicines with an alchohol base can stain fabrics. Treat in the same way as alcohol spills (see Alcohol).

To remove from carpets, blot up immediately with a clean hand cloth or tissues. Do not rub or scrub, as this will only work it deeper into the pile. Use carpet shampoo as directed by the manufacturer or detergent suds — 1 teaspoon (5 ml) to 1 cup (250 ml) warm water — gently scrubbed into the pile with a brush. Blot up as you work, and persist until the stain fades. Some medicine stains will require the services of a professional cleaner.

For medicine stains on furniture, blot up as quickly as possible. Treat as for *alcohol*.

MILDEW

Mildew is a visible fungus found in warm, humid, dark conditions. The best way to avoid mildew is to be sure things are perfectly dry before they are put away.

The microscopically small spores of mildew and mold multiply astronomically when they settle on natural materials such as paper, wool, cotton, leather, and wood, and soiled areas of synthetic fabrics.

To counter mildew attack, do not crowd clothing in a hanging space. Allow air to circulate. Store only thoroughly clean clothing.

Clean leather goods such as bags, belts, travel accessories, and shoes, and leave them in strong sunlight for an hour before wrapping them in brown paper or newspaper or storing them in cardboard boxes. Do not store these items in plastic bags; plastic will absorb leather dyes, leaving the articles irremediably stained.

Check items frequently during a long spell of damp humid weather. A musty smell emanating from a closet or cupboard is always suspect.

Remove the contents of the cupboard, vacuum well, and spray for insect control. Then place a trouble-light in the wardrobe for 2 hours. The heat it generates will dry the interior. Or use a hair dryer on wood joints and corners where mildew spores could lodge.

Silica gel or camphor blocks can be placed in musty enclosures to absorb moisture.

To remove mildew, try simple measures first. Some light spots wash out when the article is laundered. If mildew covers the article, and the article will tolerate bleach, soak it in household chlorine bleach — 2 tablespoons (30 ml) to 1 gallon (4 liters) of cold water —

Bleaching

Rub mildew spots with lemon juice and salt, and keep moist in strong sunlight until spots fade. Diluted peroxide or vinegar can be used in the same way.

Always test the effect of bleaching agents on an inconspicuous area to see if color bleaching might occur. To avoid undue fading of the rest of the garment, expose only the part being treated.

From: _____
_____
_____

BUSINESS REPLY MAIL

FIRST CLASS MAIL   PERMIT NO. 2   POWNAL, VT

POSTAGE WILL BE PAID BY ADDRESSEE

STOREY'S BOOKS FOR COUNTRY LIVING
STOREY COMMUNICATIONS, INC.
105 SCHOOLHOUSE ROAD
POWNAL VT 05261-9988

We'd love your thoughts...

Your reactions, criticisms, things you did or didn't like about this Storey Book. Please use space below (or write a letter if you'd prefer — even send photos!) telling how you've made use of the information . . . how you've put it to work . . . the more details the better! Thanks in advance for your help in building our library of good Storey Books.

Pamela B. Art

Publisher

Book Title: _____

Purchased From: _____

Comments: _____

_____

_____

_____

_____

_____

_____

Your Name: _____

Address: _____

☐ Please check here if you'd like our latest Storey's Books for Country Living Catalog.

☐ You have my permission to quote from my comments, and use these quotations in ads, brochures, mail, and other promotions used to market your books.

Signed _____ Date _____

email=Feedback@Storey.Com

PRINTED IN USA   1/96

provided the fabric has not been treated to make it drip-dry, wash-and-wear, crease-resistant, and so on. Chlorine bleach reacts on these special finishes and causes yellow-brown stains.

Mildew stains on some fabrics can be removed by moistening the stained area with lemon juice and salt, then leaving the item to dry in the sun. (It would be wise to test this cleaning solution on an inconspicuous area of the item first.)

Winter clothes. Sometimes winter suits and other clothing are put away in a packed wardrobe without being cleaned. In damp or humid weather, soil marks on these garments will become mildewed or moldy. Either causes rapid deterioration of the fabric. Rush these garments to a drycleaner.

Leather. Take mildewed leather outside and brush off powdery deposits with a clothes brush. (Stand the brush bristle down in a diluted bleach solution for 10 minutes and allow it to dry thoroughly in the sun before using on clean clothing.)

To remove surface mildew from leather, wipe the leather with a solution of equal parts rubbing alcohol and water.

Carpets. To remove mildew from carpets, first kill the fungus with a solution of 1 teaspoon (5 ml) disinfectant cleaner and 1 cup (250 ml) water. Apply to mildew and blot. Then, to remove the mildew stain, apply a mixture of ammonia and water — 1 part ammonia and 10 parts water. Blot, rinse, and vacuum when dry. It is important to dry carpets as quickly as possible; do not walk on wet pile.

Painted walls and cement paths. Use 1 part household bleach to 5 parts cold water to remove black mold from painted walls and cement paths. Leave the solution on the surface for a few minutes, then hose it off. If repainting a mold prone area of the house, use an anti fungal paint.

MILK AND CREAM

Rinse under a cold water tap. Soak in cool detergent suds or in a pre-wash enzyme solution. Wash as usual, but in cool water; hot water will set stains. If greasy marks remain, sponge with drycleaning fluid over a thick pad; air and wash again.

For washable fabrics stained with milk, sponge with cool water. Let sit, then wash in cool water. Air dry. For drycleanables, sponge with neutral detergent solution and a few drops of ammonia (unless it is silk or wool), then cool water.

To remove from carpets, scrape up as much as possible with a spatula or knife. Sponge with tepid laundry detergent suds. Avoid excessive wetting and blot with tissues as you work. Sponge with damp cloths; if a greasy mark still exists, then sponge with drycleaning fluid, being careful not to wet the backing if it is rubber, or make a paste of borax and water and work that into the pile. When the paste dries, vacuum the area.

MUD

For mud stains on washable fabrics, allow mud to thoroughly dry, then brush away loose dirt. Wash in warm water.

For drycleanables, sponge with neutral detergent solution, then rinse with water.

For really stubborn mud stains, sponge with equal parts of rubbing alcohol and water. For red earth mud stains, try rust remover (see Rust).

Never treat a wet mud stain beyond carefully lifting off the solid matter with a knife or spatula. Allow the stain to dry. When the mud stain is dry, remove the attachment from the vacuum cleaner hose and concentrate the suction pipe over the area. Then sponge out the remaining stain using warm detergent suds, 1 teaspoonful (5 ml) of powdered detergent in 1 cup (250 ml) of water. Sponge and blot repeatedly, then mop with clean, damp cloths.

MUSTARD

The turmeric in mustard is a bright yellow spice that stains. Remove as much of the loose material as possible. Flex the fabric to break up embedded residue. Apply glycerin and let it sit before washing. Hydrogen peroxide can sometimes remove mustard stains. ***Note:*** Avoid ammonia or heat — they will set the stain.

Another method is to rub undiluted detergent into dry fabric, or dampen and rub in powdered detergent. Scrub lightly between both thumbs. Rinse under cold running water. If a stain remains, soak in a pre-wash solution.

Have nonwashables drycleaned.

To remove mustard stains from a countertop, rub in a little baking soda with a damp cloth.

NAIL POLISH

To remove nail polish from carpets, blot up as much as possible with a tissue or anything handy. Then test the effect of nail polish remover on an inconspicuous part of the carpet. If there are no ill effects on the pile, apply it with an eye dropper, blotting up immediately. Sponge with warm powdered detergent suds, 1 teaspoon (5 ml) to 1 cup (250 ml) warm water. Sponge and blot many times. If a trace of color remains, make the spot as dry as possible. Slip a number of folded tissues under the stain and sponge it with nail polish remover. Change the tissue pad frequently. ***Note:*** Acetone or nail polish remover should not be used on acetates.

Any remaining dye stain can be bleached with peroxide. Keep the stain damp with diluted peroxide and expose it to sunlight.

Nonwashables should be drycleaned.

Another way to remove nail polish from carpets is to apply drycleaning fluid. Use caution if the carpet has rubber or synthetic backing. For persistent stains, mix 1 teaspoon (5 ml) mild detergent, 1 teaspoon (5 ml) white vinegar, and 1 quart (liter) warm water. Apply to stain, let dry, then vacuum.

OIL. *See also Grease and Oil*

Blot up excess oil as quickly as possible. Be gentle; forceful scrubbing will just embed the oil in the fibers. For washable fabrics, wash in as hot a water as the fabric will tolerate.

For drycleanables, rub a small amount of petroleum jelly on the stain and let it sit for 10 minutes. Take to the drycleaner as soon as possible.

PAINT

Latex paint on washables can be removed with soap and water. It is important to work on removing the paint before it dries.

To remove latex paint from carpets, scrape up as much as possible. Sponge with laundry detergent suds, 1 teaspoon (5 ml) to 1 cup (250 ml) water, blotting up as you work. Sponge with a series of clean, damp cloths to remove the suds, then with drycleaning fluid, being careful not to saturate the carpet backing. Professional help might be necessary.

Oil-based paints. Act at once. Old stains that have dried are often impossible to remove. Read the paint label, which often recommends a solvent that acts as a thinner. This is usually effective, provided a pre-testing of an inside seam shows that the fabric is not adversely affected by its use.

If expensive solvents need to be purchased, do not delay. Take the garment to a drycleaner. Supply the name of the paint or varnish involved.

Turpentine is a good paint solvent. Work from the back of the stain, which should be spread over a thick pad of tissues or folded cloth. Tamp the stain with an old nylon-bristled toothbrush dipped in turpentine. (Do not use turpentine on Arnel.)

When no more color appears on the pad under the stain, rub detergent into the area, still dampened with turpentine. Cover the stained part with hot water and let it soak for 10–12 hours. Then scrub between your thumbs and wash in the usual way.

Water-soluble paints can be rinsed out of fabrics, just as brushes can be washed in water. Rub detergent into the stain, scrub between your thumbs, rinse under running water, and wash in the usual way.

Removing oil-based paint and varnish from carpet is usually a job for a professional, but you can help by immediately scraping up as much as possible with a spatula, taking care not to spread the stain.

Sponge with thinners or turpentine, after first testing the reaction of either on an unseen section of the carpet. Try not to penetrate to the backing of the carpet; some backings will be adversely affected. Blot repeatedly to absorb as much of the loosened paint as possible.

Then sponge lightly with drycleaning fluid, blotting and sponging until the tissues remain clean. Next, gently sponge the pile with powdered detergent solution — 1 teaspoon (5 ml) dissolved in 1 cup (250 ml) tepid water; then sponge with a series of clean, damp cloths. Smooth the pile. Vacuum when quite dry.

PENCIL

Lead pencil stains on fabrics can often be removed by rubbing with a clean, soft eraser or a sponge with carbon tetrachloride. If necessary, spray with a pre-wash stain remover.

PERFUME

To remove perfume from carpet, first blot up. Sponge with laundry detergent solution, 1 teaspoon (5 ml) mixed into 1 cup (250 ml) tepid water, then with a series of damp cloths to remove the suds. Vacuum when dry. Perfume might yellow with age, so do not ignore spills.

PERSPIRATION

Perspiration will weaken fabrics, so treat vulnerable areas carefully. Dampen the stains with warm water and rub in detergent, or soak in a pre-wash soaking compound. Wash in the usual way. If the color of the fabric has been changed by perspiration, try ammonia or white vinegar to restore it. Sponge fresh stains with ammonia and immediately rinse in cold water.

Perspiration stains on upholstery result in fading, bleaching, yellowing, and greasy marks. A vinegar solution can also be used quite safely. To each cupful (250 ml) of tepid water, add 2 teaspoons (10 ml) vinegar. Wring out a cloth in the solution, and sponge briskly.

Sponging with drycleaning fluid also helps. If the cover is textured, rub this in with a soft, clean nailbrush. Blot up as much as possible with absorbent cloths. After the drycleaning fluid evaporates, apply the vinegar treatment.

Vinegar water helps to revive fading colors, and it brightens upholstery after the use of drycleaning fluids.

RUST

Rust stains on fabric can sometimes be taken out with lemon juice and salt. Apply the mixture directly to the stain and let it sit for a few minutes. Then pour boiling water through the fabric until the stain is out. Afterwards, wash as usual.

Fabrics that can be boiled can be treated in a cream of tartar solution. Use 1 tablespoon (15 ml) to 1 quart (liter) water and boil for 10 minutes or longer. Rinse well.

Clean rust from countertops with lemon juice and salt, or rub in toothpaste with your finger. Rub until the stain is gone, then rinse and wipe dry.

To remove rust stains from a slate sink, use full-strength white vinegar.

If metal furniture has accumulated rust, try scrubbing with turpentine.

SALAD DRESSING

To remove from carpet, absorb as much of the spill as possible. Mix 1 teaspoon (5 ml) mild detergent, 1 teaspoon (5 ml) white vinegar, and 1 quart (liter) warm water. Apply to stain, let dry, then vacuum. Repeat if necessary.

SALT

To clean salt marks off boots and shoes, wipe down with a mixture of 1 part white vinegar and 3 parts water.

Dry salt can change the color of a carpet and will attract dampness, which will suspend grime and dirt. If a spill occurs, vacuum slowly and deeply.

For salt water or salty liquids, blot up as much as possible. Make a solution using 1 tablespoon (15 ml) laundry detergent, 1 tablespoon (15 ml) white vinegar, and 1 cup (250 ml) tepid water. Sponge and blot several times, then sponge with damp cloths. Smooth the pile and vacuum when dry.

SCORCH MARKS. *See also Burn Marks*

Pre-test the effect of peroxide on a hidden seam as it might bleach some fabrics or react on treated materials. Dampen a cloth with hydrogen peroxide (1 part hydrogen peroxide to 3 parts water). Lay it over the scorch mark and press with a moderately hot iron. Protect surrounding material with cloth or brown paper so that it will not be scorched also. Expose to full sunshine and keep moist with peroxide until the mark fades.

Scorch marks on some fabrics are less noticeable if they are rubbed lightly with very fine sandpaper. This raises the singed nap on woolens, for example, and reduces the shiny appearance. Gentle handling of scorched garments is necessary as scorching weakens the threads.

Light scorch marks can often be bleached simply by saturating them with clean cold water and exposing them to strong sunlight.

On white materials, wet the stain with diluted hydrogen peroxide, cover with a white cloth, and press with a moderately hot iron. If a stain remains, wet again with peroxide and keep moist for 2 or 3 hours in strong sunlight. Rinse thoroughly to remove traces of peroxide.

On white or colorfast materials, wet the scorch with lemon juice and expose to sunshine. Rewet with lemon juice every half hour until the mark fades. Rinse well under running water.

Actual charring might occur when woolens and heavy synthetic materials are scorched. The nap is burnt and the threads are weakened. Remember not to abrade, rub, or twist the scorch-weakened fabric.

Light scorches on trousers might respond to treatment with a paste made of borax and glycerin. Cover the scorch mark completely and let the paste dry for 12 hours before brushing it off. Wash in tepid suds and rinse well. If the glycerin leaves an oily stain, sponge this out in warm detergent suds.

When deep scorching occurs on expensive items or garments made of wool, take the garments to a good tailor. Usually these experts can patch in a matching piece of fabric cut from a turned-up cuff or from the inside facing of a coat. The repair is almost invisible, and the cost is negligible when compared with that of replacement.

Treat scorch marks on pure silk with a paste of baking soda and cold water. When the paste dries, brush it off and repeat if necessary. Rinse well. On white silk the peroxide treatment will remove a light scorch. Rinse well.

You can also cover the mark with a thick paste made of borax and warm water. Work it into the pile. When this dries, vacuum the area and sponge with a damp cloth; vacuum again.

SCRATCHES

Scratches on furniture can often be completely camouflaged with patient treatment. Treat as you would burn marks.

SCUFF MARKS

To clean scuff marks off shoes, wipe with toothpaste on a damp rag.

SEWING MACHINE OIL

After oiling a sewing machine, remove the thread from the needle and run the machine over an old piece of cloth before sewing good material.

If machine oil does stain a garment in the making, immediately blot the spot with a tissue or rub it with chalk or talcum powder. Then, working over several folded tissues, which will act as an absorbent pad, sponge the mark with eucalyptus or drycleaning fluid.

SHOE POLISH

Work laundry detergent into the fabric immediately and rinse. For persistent stains, sponge with alcohol and rinse again, or try turpentine or cleaning fluid. Test these solutions on an inconspicuous area of the item first.

Shoe polish is dye in an oily base. Water or heat or wet spotters will spread and set the stain. Rub in vegetable oil or mineral oil and let sit for 15 minutes. Sponge in a few drops of ammonia (unless the fabric is silk or wool). If the stain is old and dry, apply petroleum jelly and wait 30 minutes.

Hair spray can be used to remove shoe polish stains from clothing (again, test on an inconspicuous area of the item first). Spray directly onto the stain, let sit for a few minutes, then wipe off gently.

To remove from carpets, lift off any solid matter with a knife or spatula. Apply drycleaning fluid drop by drop, blotting rapidly so that it does not penetrate to the backing. Exercise particular caution if the backing is made of rubber or synthetic rubber. Continue until most of the color has been removed. Then scrub the area with laundry detergent suds and an old toothbrush, working in a rotary motion from the outside of the stain toward its center. Sponge with a series of damp cloths to remove further traces.

If a blotchy mark remains after the area has dried, work carpet shampoo or a thick paste of borax and water into the pile. Allow it to remain for 4 hours before vacuuming. Repeat as necessary.

Liquid shoe polish. On carpets, blot up immediately with anything handy. Dissolve 1 teaspoon (5 ml) of laundry detergent in ½ cup (125 ml) of warm water and work this into the pile, blotting very frequently. Remaining dye stains on a

Stain Removal Kit

Fill a basket with any of the items you might need in a stain emergency. Some suggestions include white absorbent cloths and a spoon or butter knife to scrape away the spill. Include small bottles of the following stain removers:

- ☞ Drycleaning fluid
- ☞ Hydrogen peroxide
- ☞ Rubbing alcohol
- ☞ White vinegar
- ☞ Ammonia
- ☞ Diluted bleach
- ☞ Acetone

Keep the basket in a handy place, so when you are faced with a spill you won't lose time collecting materials.

light carpet might respond to bleach treatment. Mix 1 teaspoon (5 ml) in bleach with ¼ cup (60 ml) cold water and scrub this gently into the stained area with an old toothbrush, blotting frequently as you work. Finally, sponge with damp cloths to remove all traces of bleach.

SMOKE STAIN

To neutralize the odor of smoke in nonwashable items, sprinkle the item with baking soda and seal it in a plastic bag for several days. For washable items, use a baking soda and water pre-soak.

SOFT DRINKS. *See also Cola*

Soft drinks that have been spilled should be blotted up quickly, and if possible, the stain should be treated before it dries. These stains may be invisible when they dry, but they will yellow with age and heat.

Sponge immediately with a cloth barely dampened with warm water and containing 1 or 2 drops of liquid detergent. Rinse with a clean, damp cloth and dry as quickly as possible, using a hair dryer set on medium heat.

To remove from carpets, absorb as much of the spill as possible. Some drinks contain dyes that can permanently stain carpets. Mix 1 teaspoon (5 ml) mild detergent, 1 teaspoon (5 ml) white vinegar, and 1 quart (liter) warm water. Apply to stain, let dry, then vacuum. Repeat if necessary.

SOOT

To remove from carpets, vacuum lightly by holding the vacuum extension immediately above the deposits. Do not use a pushing-pulling movement. Most traces should disappear. Carpet shampoo (used according to directions), powdered carpet cleaner, or a paste made of borax and water rubbed into the pile and left to dry before vacuuming should remove any residue.

STICKERS

Stickers can sometimes be removed by applying vinegar directly or on a cloth dampened with vinegar. On nonabsorbent surfaces like glass and plastic, stickers are harder to remove. Nail polish remover, turpentine, and pre-wash spray are among the most effective.

Wet cotton with the solvent and apply it liberally over the sticker. Foil stickers do not absorb, so the solvent should be brushed around the edges. Leave for a minute or two, then repeat once or twice. The sticker can usually be peeled off. A smear of solvent will generally remove adhesive.

A light application of pre-wash spray will usually remove adhesive left by sticky tape, particularly from walls where posters have been hung. It will also remove masking tape marks from around glass after window frames have been painted.

Commercial jar labels can usually be soaked off except for a strip of adhesive that attaches to the ends. Many jars are purposely designed for re-use so they need to be clear of old labels. Try one of the suggested solvents or the pre-wash spray to remove final traces. Always work in a well-ventilated area when using spray.

TAR

Lift off as much solid matter as possible immediately, using a knife to do so. Spread the stain over a thick pad of face tissues and tamp the stain with an old toothbrush dipped in eucalyptus. As the tissues become stained, discard them and substitute new ones. Finally, spread the stain over a plate or saucer, pour over a little more eucalyptus oil, and continue to tamp or gently scrape the area with a blunt knife. Blot up stained matter, and rinse the saucer. Repeat until no more tar can be extracted.

If eucalyptus is not available, use turpentine, carbon tetrachloride, or drycleaning fluid.

Dried tar. Soften with warmed olive oil after spreading the stain over folded tissues. Then proceed as above, preferably using eucalyptus oil as the solvent.

Rub detergent into the stain, rub between both thumbs, and rinse under running water as hot as the hands can bear. If a yellow mark remains, bleach it by keeping it moist with peroxide and exposing it to full sunlight. Rinse well.

Have nonwashable garments drycleaned as soon as possible.

To remove from carpets, lift off solid matter with a knife. If the tar has dried, it will need to be softened with warmed oil. Put a few drops on the tar and leave it until the tar feels soft to the touch. Then use tissues to blot up excess oil.

Sponge carefully with eucalyptus or with turpentine. To avoid spreading the stain, continually blot the area with tissues, which will absorb loosened tar elements.

Sponge with laundry detergent solution — 1 teaspoon (5 ml) to ½ cup (125 ml) warm water. If the tar is trodden into the pile, scrub with a toothbrush. Continue to scrub and blot for as long as tissues continue to be stained with brown sulphur traces from the tar; then sponge with a series of damp cloths. Use drycleaning fluid to remove traces of oil used to soften the tar; if these remain, they will attract grime. Blot frequently as you work.

Concentrated cleaning such as this might result in a very clean patch of carpet with grimier surroundings. Shampooing the whole carpet may prove necessary.

TEA

If hot or boiling water can be flushed through a fresh tea stain, the stain will fade. If the fabric involved can stand boiling or very hot water, spread the stain over a large basin in the sink. Cover the mark with borax. Pour a jug or kettleful of boiling water over the stain. Let it soak in the water until it cools. You can also turn on a hot water tap. Hold the stained area taut beneath its flow; often the stain will be washed out.

Lemon juice and sunlight also will bleach tannin stains. Rub lemon juice into the marks, and hang or spread them in full sunlight. Keep moist with lemon juice, perhaps for two days, until the stains fade. Rinse well and wash.

On colored fabrics, treat tea stains with a borax paste. Mix 1 tablespoon (15 ml) of borax to a paste with hot water. Spread it over the stain. When this dries, brush it off and apply fresh paste. Continue until the mark fades; or if it persists, apply diluted peroxide and expose to sunlight, keeping it damp for several hours.

Tea spilled on woolens or on blankets should be mopped up as quickly as possible. Send lined garments to a drycleaner. Rinse a stained blanket in warm detergent suds and in a succession of warm rinsing waters. If a tea stain has dried on a blanket, soak it in a hydrogen peroxide solution. To each tablespoon (15 ml) of hydrogen peroxide, add 5 tablespoons (75 ml) warm water. Wet the tea stain thoroughly. Let the blanket soak until the stain fades; then wash the entire blanket, or rinse that section very well and roll it in a towel or blot it semi-dry before drying it completely.

Glycerin will reconstitute an old tea stain, making it easier to remove. Rub in glycerin, working it in with a scrubbing action between both thumbs. Leave it on for 10 hours. Then spread the stain over a basin in the sink, cover it with borax, and pour over it water as hot as the fabric can stand. Let it soak in the borax solution until the mark fades. (See also Coffee and Tea.)

UNKNOWN MATERIALS

Depending on the fabric or material that is stained, you may want to try one of the following stain removal techniques.

➤ Blot with cool water.

➤ Blot with a wet sponge on which you have sprinkled a few drops of vinegar. (Do not use this on cotton or linen.)

➤ Blot with a wet sponge on which you have sprinkled a few drops of ammonia. (Do not use this on cotton or linen.)

➤ Blot with rubbing alcohol that has been diluted with an equal amount of water. Rinse well.

➤ Sponge with a solution of bleach and water.

URINE

Fresh stains are comparatively easy to remove. First rinse well, pre-soak using an enzyme powder or powdered detergent in the water, then wash in the usual way. Or sponge immediately with salty water; later rinse well and wash in the usual way. If the color of the fabric has been changed, sponge the mark with ammonia, then rinse again. (Do not use ammonia on wool or silk.) Yellow stains on white materials such as cotton sheets can be soaked in chlorine bleach. Do not use bleach on materials with treated finishes that make them no-iron or wash-and-wear. Bleach will cause yellow-brown marks on specially treated fabrics.

Soak urine-stained fabrics in clear water for 30 minutes (hot water is best, if the care label permits). Add detergent, wash, then rinse. If necessary, use a bleach that is safe for the fabric. If fabric color changes, sponge with ammonia. If the stain remains, sponge with white vinegar. Launder again.

A mixture of white vinegar and baking soda is a good neutralizer. Sponge onto fabric or carpet.

To remove from carpets, blot up quickly so that as little as possible is absorbed. Prepare a solution of 2 teaspoons (10 ml) powdered laundry detergent, ¼ cup

(125 ml) warm water, and 2 tablespoons (30 ml) white vinegar. Scrub this into the pile of the carpet, using an old toothbrush. Let it remain for 20 minutes, then sponge repeatedly with clean, damp cloths.

Urine stains darken with age, and they can bleach dark carpets. Sometimes the color can be restored by sponging with ammonia water. Use 1 teaspoon (5 ml) ammonia in a cup (250 ml) of cold water. It is advisable to first test the effect of ammonia on an inconspicuous part of the carpet before sponging a large area. After the ammonia treatment, sponge with a series of clean, damp cloths.

Pet and some baby urine will leave a recurring odor, particularly in damp or humid weather or if a room has been closed up. Drugstores stock solutions that can be used to deodorize as well as remove stains. Most can be sprayed on. For persistent odors, turn back the carpet and clean and spray the backing and underlay.

VOMIT

To remove from carpets, attend to this stain without delay. Use a spatula to remove solid matter and an old towel to blot up as much as possible. Prepare a sponging solution using 1 tablespoon (15 ml) laundry detergent in 1 cup (250 ml) warm water, plus 1 tablespoon (15 ml) white vinegar. Scrub into the area with a nailbrush. Try to avoid overwetting. If saturation results, the wet carpet backing will absorb some of the unpleasant odor, which will be difficult to remove.

After traces of detergent have been sponged out with a series of damp cloths, use drycleaning fluid to remove greasy deposits. Blot persistently to absorb as much moisture as possible. Finally, sponge with dry towels and train an electric fan or hair dryer on the area to dry the carpet. Vacuum when dry.

WATER

An overflowing bath or basin, a leaking pipe, a storm-damaged roof, even a knocked-over vase can cause severe carpet stains. Copious amounts of water will loosen grime and dirt deposits; the backing and underlay become saturated and the carpet is stained with dirty marks. In addition to the shrinking that can be caused by saturation, some underlays will mildew and the resulting smell is very unpleasant. Some carpet dyes might bleed; others might fade.

Absorb as much water as possible with bath towels. Walk on them to press them deeply into the pile where they will absorb still more water.

The best course of action in the event of severe flooding is to take up the carpet and dry it out or to turn back the carpet to the saturated section and train an electric fan on the backing until it is dry. Never use a radiator; synthetic carpets scorch easily, and woolen carpets will shrink.

If the carpet is a good one, have it steam-cleaned by a professional carpet cleaner. It will also need to be relaid by a professional, who might need to stretch a shrunken wall-to-wall carpet.

Water rings on furniture. Damp marks on furniture are often caused by leaking vases and rings of condensation from cold glasses. The polish must be removed so that the area can be buffed dry. Put a little vinegar on a damp cloth and wipe the wet mark. It will remove the old polish and darken the bleached wood. Dry well, then work in linseed oil or petroleum jelly. Rub hard from the outside of the mark toward the center. Cover with more oil or petroleum jelly, and leave for several hours before again rubbing with a heated duster. A duster can be warmed by standing a heating iron on it for a minute or two. The warmth will help the wood absorb the oil. Then polish in the usual way; or, if the mark remains, repeat the rubbing treatment.

WINE

Treat as soon as possible. On a garment, spray or sponge with carbonated soda water. On a cloth, sprinkle heavily with salt after blotting up as much as possible. Later, follow instructions for removing tea stains. (See Tea.)

Do not hesitate to send an expensive garment to a drycleaner.

On upholstery, immediately blot up as much as possible. Sponge with warm water; blot and sponge repeatedly. Cover the stain with a dry tissue and sprinkle this with talcum powder. Cover with another tissue and apply a weight. The tissues and the powder will absorb still more of the stain. Lift off carefully. Vacuum.

To remove red wine stains from carpets, dilute the stain with white wine, then clean the spot with cold water and cover with salt. Wait 15 minutes, then vacuum up the salt.

Another method for removing wine from carpets is first to blot it up immediately, then spray with effervescing soda water. Blot persistently. Make a thick paste of borax and warm water, and scrub it deeply into the carpet pile with a nailbrush or toothbrush. Let it remain overnight before vacuuming. Repeat several times if necessary.

YELLOW SPOTS AND STAINS

Sometimes caused by soap residue (especially in linens that are ironed). Treat the stains in the following way: Apply fresh lemon juice on stains, then sprinkle the juice with salt. Stretch the fabric tightly and pour hot water through the stains.

Tablet denture cleaners will remove yellow stains from fabrics. Fill container with warm water and add cleaning tablets according to the directions on the box. After tablets dissolve, add the stained item and soak until stain comes out.

If the exterior of a white freezer or refrigerator has yellowed with age, apply an automotive cutting compound, available from garages or hardware stores.

APPENDIX

Product Assistance

The U.S. Consumer Product and Safety Commission has a toll-free number, **1-800-638-2772**. To obtain information for a commercial product, you can check the product label or ask your local library for the address and telephone number of the manufacturer. Call manufacturers for information about specific products.

Poison Information

Contact your local poison center about the health effect of products and for information about treating poisoning. The telephone number for poison control usually appears on the inside cover of your telephone directory.

HOUSEHOLD HAZARDOUS WASTE REFERENCE

SUBSTANCE ☞	PROBLEM ☞
Bleach and liquid cleaners	Contain strong oxidizers. Can cause burns.
Cleansers and powdered cleaners	Contain strong oxidizers. Poisonous. Can cause burns.
Drain cleaners	Poisonous. Can cause serious burns. May contain carcinogens.
Dyes	Poisonous, especially to children; don't use cooking utensils when dyeing. May be carcinogenic.
Furniture polishes	Include various poisonous solvents. One ounce (25 grams) may be lethal to an adult.
Mothballs	Contain poisonous chemical compounds.
Oven cleaners	Poisonous. Can cause serious burns. May contain carcinogens.
Silver polishes	Poisonous. May contain carcinogens. One ounce (25 grams) may be lethal to an adult.
Spot removers	Poisonous. Most are solvent-based. May be carcinogenic.
Toilet cleaners	Spray cans are the most dangerous. Poisonous. Can cause serious burns. One teaspoonful (5 ml) may be lethal to an adult.
Window cleaners	Contain harmful chemical compounds and sometimes carcinogens. May cause birth defects.

PROPER DISPOSAL ☞	ALTERNATIVES
Wash down drain with lots of water.	Use powder, not liquid bleach.
Wrap tightly in plastic, place in a box, tape shut, and put in garbage.	Baking soda and mild detergent, elbow grease.
Wash down drain with lots of water or take to hazardous waste collection site.	Boiling water, plunger, metal snake.
Wrap tightly in plastic, place in a box, tape shut, and put in garbage.	Use vegetable dyes such as onion skins, teas, marigolds.
Use up according to directions or take to hazardous waste collection site.	Mineral oil with lemon oil (but this may strip finish), or Carnauba wax.
Use up according to directions or take to hazardous waste collection site.	Cedar chips, newspapers; wrap wool clothing in plastic bags during warm seasons.
Use up according to directions or take to hazardous-waste collection site.	Salt, quarter cup (60 ml) of ammonia overnight.
Use up according to directions or take to hazardous waste collection site.	Soak silver in water with baking soda, salt, and small piece of aluminum foil.
Use up according to directions or take to hazardous waste collection site.	Immediate cold water and detergent, rubbing alcohol, or a little acetone.
Wash down drain with lots of water.	Mild detergent or small amounts of bleach.
Wrap tightly in plastic, place in a box, tape shut, and put in garbage.	Vinegar and water

SOURCE: League of Women Voters of Marin County, California. Used with permission. For further information, contact your local solid waste authority.

REFERENCES

Aslett, Don. *Stainbuster's Bible.* Penguin, 1990.

Barndt, Herb. *Professor Barndt's On-the-Spot Stain Removal Guide.* Doubleday, 1992.

Barrott, Patti. *Too Busy to Clean? Over 500 Tips & Techniques to Make Housecleaning Easier.* Storey Publishing, 1990.

Berthold-Bond, Annie. *Clean & Green: The Complete Guide to Non-Toxic & Environmentally Safe Housekeeping.* Ceres Press, 1990.

Chestnut Moore, Alma. *How to Clean Everything.* Simon & Schuster, 1977.

Consumer Guide, ed. *Practical Hints & Tips.* Consumer Guide, 1994.

Pinkham, Mary Ellen, and Pearl Higginbotham. *Mary Ellen's Best of Helpful Hints.* Warner, 1979.

Proux, Earl. *Yankee Home Hints.* Yankee Books, 1993.

Time Life Staff. *Cleaning & Stain Removal.* Time Life, 1990.

INDEX